Know It, Show It

GRADE 4

Printed in the U.S.A.

ISBN   978-0-358-19209-1

11 12 13 14   0909   26 25 24 23

4500865823

r7.20

Grade 4

Contents

Name _____

Short *a* and Long *a*

▶ **Read each sentence. Find the word that includes the short or long *a* vowel sound. Underline the vowel or vowel team that makes the sound. After the sentence, underline "Short *a* Sound" or "Long *a* Sound."**

1. Did Josh sprain his knee running?

        Short *a* Sound   Long *a* Sound

2. If I make an error in spelling, I just erase it.

        Short *a* Sound   Long *a* Sound

3. This bread is stale.

        Short *a* Sound   Long *a* Sound

4. Mr. Green will remain with the children.

        Short *a* Sound   Long *a* Sound

5. He used a firm grasp to open the jar.

        Short *a* Sound   Long *a* Sound

6. I was amazed that I could climb the rope.

        Short *a* Sound   Long *a* Sound

7. Mom took a break from grilling dinner.

        Short *a* Sound   Long *a* Sound

8. Josie cleaned the drain with vinegar.

        Short *a* Sound   Long *a* Sound

9. We built a strong raft from the wood.

        Short *a* Sound   Long *a* Sound

Name _____

Critical Vocabulary

▶ **Use your understanding of the Critical Vocabulary words to support your answers to the questions below.**

1. How would you feel if someone treated you with **disdain**?

_____

_____

2. What might you do **inadvertently** while listening to a **mundane** person speak?

_____

_____

3. What are some things that cannot be **consumed**?

_____

_____

4. Tell about a time you **considered** something before you **obliged** to do it.

_____

_____

5. Tell about a time you acted in **defiance**.

_____

_____

6. What are ways you may have **descended** from the second floor to the first floor?

_____

_____

7. What is something **profound** you could say to someone you care about?

_____

_____

8. If you were planning a party outside, what might a **cynic** expect to happen?

_____

_____

▶ **Choose two of the Critical Vocabulary words and use them in a sentence.**

_____

_____

_____

_____

_____

Name _____

Author's Purpose

Knowing the **author's purpose** can help you understand the author's message and main idea.

> **Answer the questions in *Flora and Ulysses: The Illuminated Adventures*.**

1. What is the author's purpose for writing *Flora and Ulysses*?

_____

_____

2. What parts of the text support your answer?

_____

_____

> **Answer the questions about page 38 in *Flora and Ulysses: The Illuminated Adventures*.**

3. What message does the author want to share?

_____

_____

_____

4. How do the characters and story events help you understand the message?

_____

_____

_____

Name _____

Words with Short and Long a

> Use the words from the box to complete the spelling patterns chart for short and long *a*.

quake	class	past	delay
amaze	gray	grasp	break
steak	apple	fail	
plate	grape	crayon	

Short *a* Vowel Sound	Long *a* Vowel Sound/ Open Syllable	Long Vowel/ Consonant/Silent Vowel	Two Vowel Team/ Long Vowel Sound
closed (*last*)	open (*maybe*)	VCe (*blade*)	vowel team (*stain*)

> Pick one word from each column and use it in a sentence. Write the sentences on the lines below.

1. _____

2. _____

3. _____

4. _____

Name _____

Prefixes un–, in–, im–, re–

> Complete the chart with words that contain the prefixes *un–*, *in–*, *im–*, *re–*.

un–	in–	im–	re–

> Write a sentence for each word in the chart.

_____

_____

_____

_____

_____

_____

_____

_____

_____

_____

Name _____

Text and Graphic Features

Text and graphic features, such as the style and the size of print, can help tell a story or make information clear. Some texts include special type that looks different from the other words on the page. Using special type draws attention to a particular idea, event, or situation.

▶ **Use pages 20–21 in** *Flora and Ulysses: The Illuminated Adventures* **to answer the questions below.**

1. What do you learn through the words and images on pages 20–21?

   _____

   _____

   _____

2. Why might the author have used a graphic novel format to begin the story?

   _____

   _____

   _____

▶ **Revisit page 28 and answer the questions below.**

3. What words on page 28 appear in special type?

   _____

   _____

4. Why do you think the author uses special type for these words?

   _____

   _____

Name _____

Figurative Language

Authors use **figurative language** to create a special effect or feeling, or they use figurative language to make a point. Figurative language includes figures of speech that compare, exaggerate, or mean something different from what is expected.

> **Read the last two sentences on page 24 in *Flora and Ulysses: The Illuminated Adventures*.**

1. How do the words *poof* and *fwump* add to the story?

_____

_____

_____

> **Reread paragraph 41 on page 26.**

2. Which part of paragraph 41 shows exaggeration through use of a hyperbole?

_____

_____

_____

3. How does the author's use of hyperbole help describe the squirrel's personality? Why did the author choose to use hyperbole here?

_____

_____

Short e and Long e

▶ Place the long *e* words in the first column and the short *e* words in the second column.

engine	complete	speck
freedom	west	greed
beast	gleam	speed
fresh	kept	shelf
cheap	member	belief

Long *e*	Short *e*

▶ Write two sentences using the words from the list. Circle the long *e* words and underline the short *e* words in your sentences.

_____

_____

_____

_____

Name _____

Critical Vocabulary

> Use your understanding of the Critical Vocabulary words to create a word web for each word. In the center is one of these words. In the outer ovals, write words and phrases that relate to that word. Discuss your word webs with a partner.

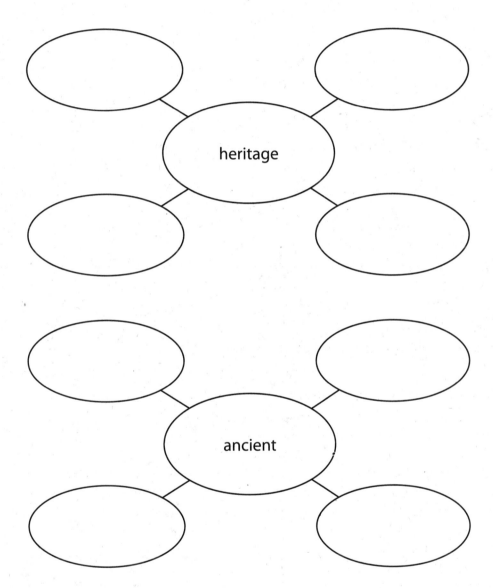

> Use the Critical Vocabulary words in sentences of your own.

_____

_____

Elements of Poetry

Narrative Poetry uses imagery and poetic language to tell a story. This type of poem includes some of the same elements of a story, such as:

- characters
- setting
- events
- a theme

▶ **Reread pages 44–45 in** *Yes! We Are Latinos* **to identify the structure of the poem and answer the question.**

1. How does the poem's structure help you understand it?

_____

_____

_____

▶ **Reread pages 46–47 and answer the question.**

2. How does the poem's structure help you understand pages 46 and 47?

_____

_____

_____

Short e and Long e

> Read each sentence. Choose a word from the word box to complete each item. Write the word on the line. Then identify the word as short *e* or long *e*.

chief	steam	member	reason
speed	west	greed	eager
sleeve	believe	steep	shelf
complete	fresh	pretend	cheap

1. Which word names a direction? _____

           Short *e* Sound   Long *e* Sound

2. A tall hill that is hard to climb is _____ .

           Short *e* Sound   Long *e* Sound

3. _____ means the opposite of stale.

           Short *e* Sound   Long *e* Sound

4. _____ means how fast something goes.

           Short *e* Sound   Long *e* Sound

5. The leader of a tribe is called _____ .

           Short *e* Sound   Long *e* Sound

6. If someone is excited to do something, they are _____ .

           Short *e* Sound   Long *e* Sound

7. Boiling water makes _____ .

           Short *e* Sound   Long *e* Sound

8. When you join a club, you become a _____ .

           Short *e* Sound   Long *e* Sound

9. A good place to put books is a _____ .

           Short *e* Sound   Long *e* Sound

Name _____

Critical Vocabulary

You can use the words you learn from reading as you talk and write.

▷ **Use your understanding of the Critical Vocabulary words to support your answers to the questions below.**

1. What is a baby elephant **relying** on its mother to do for it?

_____

2. Why don't people stick to their **resolutions**?

_____

3. Why might it be **awkward** to forget a classmate's name?

_____

_____

4. What might make a person feel **clumsy**?

_____

_____

5. What **doubts** might someone have on the first day of school?

_____

_____

▷ **Choose two of the Critical Vocabulary words and use them in a sentence.**

_____

_____

Name _____

Point of View

It's important to know from whose **point of view** the events are told. That's because different people can tell the same story different ways!

Stories are often told from a first-person or a third-person point of view.

First-Person Point of View The narrator . . .	Third-Person Point of View The narrator . . .
is a character in the story.	is someone outside the story.
tells his or her own thoughts and feelings.	tells the thoughts and feelings of others.
uses pronouns such as *I*, *me*, *my*, *mine*, and *we*.	uses pronouns such as *he*, *she*, and *they*.

▶ Reread page 58 in *The Year of the Rat* to answer the questions.

1. Who is the narrator in this part of the story? From what point of view is this part of the story told? Give examples to support your answer.

   _____

   _____

▶ Reread page 61 and think about how the point of view changes.

2. Who is the narrator in this part of the story? From what point of view is this part of the story told? Why do you think the author tells the story from this point of view now?

   _____

   _____

▶ Reread page 63 to practice determining point of view in a text.

3. What is the narrator's point of view in "Knowing the Fish"? How do you know?

   _____

Name _____

Prefixes mis-, pre-, dis-

▶ Complete the chart with words that contain the prefixes *mis–, pre–, dis–*.

mis–	pre–	dis–

▶ Write a sentence for each word in the chart.

_____

_____

_____

_____

_____

_____

_____

_____

_____

_____

_____

Name _____

Character

Characters are the people or animals in a story. As characters deal with a conflict, readers see how one event causes another event to happen and how characters find a resolution.

> **Reread page 62 in *The Year of the Rat* and identify Pacy's conflict.**

1. What is Pacy's conflict at this point of the story? How does does this conflict affect Pacy?

   _____

   _____

> **Reread page 66 to answer the following questions about Pacy's character.**

2. What reason does Pacy give for wanting to work alone? What does this action show about her?

   _____

   _____

3. What does Pacy mean when she says she will be an author and illustrator "no matter what"?

   _____

   _____

> **Reread page 69 to look for details about how Pacy's character changes.**

4. How do Pacy's thoughts about Becky and Charlotte show that she has changed?

   _____

   _____

   _____

Short *i* and Long *i*

> Sort the Spelling Words correctly. Which words have a short *i* sound, and which words have a long *i* sound?

Short *i*	Long *i*

> Complete the sentence by choosing the correct word. Write the correct word on the line.

1. A new lamp will _____ the room.

2. A strong _____ blew for hours.

3. The book club must _____ which book to read.

4. The low temperatures caused a _____ in the air.

5. There was a wide _____ on the side of the road.

6. Our town decided to _____ a new skating rink.

7. Long ago a _____ wheel was used to turn thread into cloth.

8. Beautiful handwriting requires _____.

Spelling Words

witness

skill

decide

ticket

live

brighten

spinning

sigh

ditch

build

chill

remind

inch

surprise

wind

Name _____

Critical Vocabulary

You can use the words you learn from reading as you talk and write.

▷ **Use your understanding of the Critical Vocabulary words to support your answers to the questions below. Then use the Critical Vocabulary words as you talk with a partner about your answers.**

1. When have you acted **cautiously**?

_____

_____

2. How would you feel if there was only a **trickle** of water left in your water bottle?

_____

_____

3. When have you **marveled** at something **majestic** in nature?

_____

_____

4. What should be **proclaimed** as a **mighty** feat?

_____

_____

5. What **distant** place would you like to see that you've never seen before?

_____

_____

6. What would a **sumptuous** meal have to include?

_____

_____

Name _____

7. What would you buy with a **hoard** of cash?

_____

_____

> **Write a sentence using two Critical Vocabulary words below.**

_____

_____

_____

_____

_____

Literary Elements

All stories have a certain structure. **Literary elements** such as character, plot, and setting form this structure. Elements of structure vary from story to story, though. For example, the culture in which a story is set can influence the story's plot. Also, interactions among characters and the changes they undergo influence a story.

▶ **Reread page 78 in *Kitoto the Mighty* and answer the question about the story structure.**

1. How has the author crafted the structure of the plot?

_____

_____

▶ **Reread paragraphs 17–19 of page 82 and look at the illustrations. Then answer the question about story details.**

2. What details help describe the cultural setting of the folktale?

_____

_____

▶ **Reread page 85 and answer the question about Kitoto's character.**

3. How does Kitoto's character change again when faced with the "giant"? What is the reason for this change?

_____

_____

▶ **Reread page 86 and answer the question about the story structure.**

4. How would you describe the story structure of this folktale?

_____

Name _____

Suffixes –y and –ly

> Complete the chart with words that contain the suffixes –y, –ly.

–y	–ly

> Write a sentence for each word in the chart.

_____

_____

_____

_____

_____

_____

_____

Name _____

Theme

Most stories have a **theme**, which tells the author's message. A theme might be a story's main message, a moral, or a lesson.

> ▶ **Revisit pages 82–88 and answer the question about the theme of** *Kitoto the Mighty.*

1. What has Kitoto learned from his search so far?

_____

_____

2. Why is Kitoto so sure that the most powerful being must be a giant? How does this connect to the theme?

_____

_____

_____

_____

> ▶ **Page through the folktale. Then answer the questions.**

3. What does Kitoto learn? What is the theme of this folktale?

_____

_____

_____

4. What is the author's message or lesson to be learned from this folktale? What other themes do you see in this folktale?

_____

_____

Name _____

Short *i* and Long *i*

> Read each riddle. Choose a word from the box that answers the riddle. Write the word on the line. Then underline whether the word has the short *i* or long *i* sound.

ditch	splice	chill	ticket	witness
build	brighten	inch	brick	flight

1. I am the measure you use in a pinch. I'm on rulers and yardsticks. I must be an _____ ! Short *i* Sound Long *i* Sound	**2.** I am used to make buildings tall, strong, and thick. I'm made of dried clay. I am a _____ . Short *i* Sound Long *i* Sound
3. I come in the winter and increase your heating bill. When the air's frosty and cold, I am a _____ . Short *i* Sound Long *i* Sound	**4.** When you add light into any room or space, you flip on the light switch and you _____ the place! Short *i* Sound Long *i* Sound
5. When the sun is shining and the clouds are white, you hop on an airplane and take off on your _____ . Short *i* Sound Long *i* Sound	**6.** I saw it happen. I must confess. I watched the crime. I must be the _____ . Short *i* Sound Long *i* Sound

Name _____

Author's Craft

Author's craft is the way an author uses language to share his or her ideas and make a piece of writing interesting.

▶ **Reread page 76 in *Kitoto the Mighty* and answer the questions about author's craft.**

1. How does the author use figurative language on page 76?

_____

_____

_____

2. What is the comparison that is being made? Why?

_____

_____

_____

_____

▶ **Reread page 81 and answer the question about the author's use of imagery.**

3. How does the author use imagery in this folktale? Cite an example from the text.

_____

_____

_____

_____

_____

Name _____

Short and Long o Sounds

▶ **Read each sentence. Find the word that includes the short or long o vowel sound. Underline the vowel or vowel team that makes the sound. Below the sentence, underline "Short o Sound" or "Long o Sound."**

1. The bold kitten climbed to the highest bookshelf.

       Short *o* Sound   Long *o* Sound

2. Yesterday, my lunch was a bowl of vegetable soup.

       Short *o* Sound   Long *o* Sound

3. It seems odd that the students aren't talking during recess.

       Short *o* Sound   Long *o* Sound

4. Chandra woke at sunrise and couldn't get back to sleep.

       Short *o* Sound   Long *o* Sound

5. Do you like raisins and brown sugar in oatmeal?

       Short *o* Sound   Long *o* Sound

6. My sister builds forts out of couch pillows.

       Short *o* Sound   Long *o* Sound

7. I looked at my grades online, at the school's website.

       Short *o* Sound   Long *o* Sound

8. Ken used the globe to find the Weddell Sea.

       Short *o* Sound   Long *o* Sound

9. Raj is a hero because he risks his life to help people.

       Short *o* Sound   Long *o* Sound

10. The little tot screamed with delight and ran around the playground.

        Short *o* Sound   Long *o* Sound

Name _____

Critical Vocabulary

You can use the words you learn from reading as you talk and write.

▶ **Use details from *The Science Behind Sight* to support your answers to the questions below. Then use the Critical Vocabulary words as you talk with a partner about your answers.**

1. What would happen if light did not **reflect** off solid objects?

_____

2. Which would you describe as **transparent**, a brick wall or a window? Explain.

_____

3. Why is it easier to **judge** the distance between two objects with both eyes at the front of your head?

_____

_____

4. What would you use to **illuminate** a large area?

_____

5. Would you need a **luminous** object to read a book if you were in a bright room? Why or why not?

_____

_____

▶ **Choose two of the Critical Vocabulary words and use them in a sentence.**

_____

_____

Name _____

Text and Graphic Features

Informational text often includes **text features** such as headings and boldfaced words. Informational text usually includes one or more **graphic features** such as photographs, diagrams, and illustrations.

> **Answer the questions about page 111 of *The Science Behind Sight*.**

1. How does the diagram connect to the text in the caption?

_____

_____

2. How does the diagram add to your understanding of the ideas in paragraph 16?

_____

_____

> **Choose another diagram in *The Science Behind Sight*.**

3. What does the diagram explain?

_____

_____

4. How does the diagram add to your understanding of the text?

_____

_____

Name _____

Short and Long o Sounds

> Read each sentence. Under the blank are the words "Short *o* Sound" or "Long *o* Sound." Find a word from the box that contains that vowel sound and makes sense in the sentence. Write the word in the blank.

Short *o* Sound	Long *o* Sound
frosty	bowling
lobby	grove
plodded	protested
softened	toasted

1. The school's _____ area is by the front door.
   Short *o* Sound

2. The sound in the _____ alley was like thunder.
   Long *o* Sound

3. I _____ toward the car, dragging my feet all the way.
   Short *o* Sound

4. This _____ of trees is home to lots of wildlife.
   Long *o* Sound

5. Mark _____ some bread for breakfast.
   Long *o* Sound

6. The _____ winter air felt clean and crisp.
   Short *o* Sound

7. Sara whined and _____ her early bedtime.
   Long *o* Sound

8. The butter _____ and melted under the hot sun.
   Short *o* Sound

Name _____

Latin Root *lumin*

The words *luminous* and *illuminates* contain a root that has Latin origins.
The meaning of the root *lumin* is "light."

> **Complete the chart with other words that contain the root *lumin*.**

lumin
_____
_____
_____
_____

> **Write a sentence for each word in the chart.**

_____

_____

_____

_____

_____

_____

_____

_____

_____

_____

Name _____

Text Structure

Authors use different **text structures**, or ways of organizing information in a text. Figuring out a text's structure can help you understand its important ideas.

▶ **Answer the questions about paragraphs 17–21 of** *The Science Behind Sight.*

1. What is the structure of this part of the text? How do you know?

_____

_____

_____

2. How does knowing the text's structure help you understand the central idea on these pages?

_____

_____

▶ **Revisit pages 116–117 in** *The Science Behind Sight.*

3. What is the structure on pages 116–117? How do you know?

_____

_____

_____

4. What is the text structure on page 118? How do you know?

_____

_____

5. Why do you think the author used this type of text structure here?

_____

_____

Name _____

Content-Area Words

Content-area words are words about a specific topic. Readers can figure out the meanings of these words by looking for context clues in the sentence or in the paragraph and in visuals.

▶ **Turn to page 109 of *The Science Behind Sight*.**

1. Which word is a content-area word, *eyelid* or *protect*? How can you tell?

_____

_____

2. Why is the word *iris* a content-area word?

_____

_____

3. What clues around the word *iris* help you know what *iris* means?

_____

_____

4. What clues around the word *pupil* help you know what *pupil* means?

_____

_____

▶ **Find and list the content-area words on page 109.**

Content-Area Words:

_____   _____   _____

_____   _____   _____

Syllable Division Patterns: VCCV, VCV, VV

▶ **Read each sentence. Look carefully at the underlined word. Write the underlined word in the correct column to show which syllable division pattern it follows.**

Sentence	VCCV	VCV	VV
1. There was an old trunk in the <u>attic</u>.			
2. Each year our class has a <u>poetry</u> festival.			
3. The <u>lion</u> is native to Africa.			
4. I try <u>never</u> to be late for school.			
5. A farmer uses a <u>tractor</u> to plow his fields.			
6. Our dog is a <u>rescue</u> from the shelter.			
7. The <u>dentist</u> told us to brush our teeth more often.			
8. The kitten's fur was as smooth as <u>velvet</u>.			
9. There is a <u>hotel</u> near the airport.			
10. She was in a hurry to <u>open</u> the package.			

Name _____

Critical Vocabulary

You can use the words you learn from reading as you talk and write.

≥ Use your understanding of the Critical Vocabulary words to support your answers to the questions below. Then use the Critical Vocabulary words as you talk with a partner about your answers.

1. What is something you **relish**?

_____

_____

2. What **familiar** object can't you do without?

_____

_____

3. What time of year do you **savor** most?

_____

_____

4. How might you enhance your chances of doing well on a test?

_____

_____

≥ Write a sentence using two Critical Vocabulary words below.

_____

_____

Name _____

Media Techniques

Media is the means of communication through radio, newspapers, television, magazines, and the Internet. **Media techniques** are the methods through which information is communicated. Media techniques include sound and visual elements, live action, animation, and information.

> **Answer the following questions about *Animal Senses*.**

1. How does the video help you understand more about the animal sense of hearing?

_____

_____

_____

_____

2. How does the video help you understand more about the animal sense of touch?

_____

_____

_____

_____

3. How is the video helpful in understanding more about animal sounds?

_____

_____

_____

_____

Name _____

Words with Syllable Division Patterns: VCCV, VCV, VV

▶ **Choose the word with the given syllable division pattern to complete the sentence. Write the word on the line.**

1. The riverbank was _____ and steep.   VCCV
                      muddy   wet

2. The farmer's field was full of _____.   VCV
                              wheat   clover

3. A carpenter uses a _____ in his work.   VCCV
                saw   hammer

4. The _____ took a nap in the warm sun.   VV
       tiger   lion

5. We could smell the _____ cooking in the kitchen.   VCV
                bacon   waffles

6. Our music teacher will play the _____ for our class concert.   VV
                    piano   trumpet

7. In science class, we used _____ for our experiment.   VCCV
                magnets   heat

8. She has a great _____ for high-speed transportation.   VV
          plan   idea

Name _____

Critical Vocabulary

You can use the words you learn from reading as you talk and write.

▶ **Use your understanding of the Critical Vocabulary words to support your answers to the questions below.**

1. What could happen if rules are not **accepted** by all members of a group?

_____

2. What **obstacles** might stand in the way of someone becoming an Olympic athlete?

_____

3. What is a **command** you would give to a dog?

_____

4. Why is **denying** your feelings a bad idea?

_____

5. When did you have to **adapt** to a new situation?

_____

6. Why do people feel better when they **comfort** others?

_____

▶ **Choose two of the Critical Vocabulary words and use them in a sentence.**

_____

_____

Name _____

Figurative Language

Figurative language is the use of words and phrases that create a feeling or image. The words take on meanings beyond their everyday or dictionary meanings. The chart below shows some examples.

Figurative Language	Definition	Examples
Simile	Uses the word *like* or *as* to compare two things	• She can sing like a bird! • My cat's fur is as smooth as silk.
Metaphor	Compares two things or ideas without using *like* or *as*	• His smile fills the room with sunshine. • His face was a wooden mask.
Idiom	Has a different meaning from the usual, or literal, meaning of the words	• I'm so happy, I'm walking on air! • He let the cat out of the bag and spoiled the surprise.

> ▶ Reread paragraph 3 in *Blind Ambition*. Then answer the question below.

1. What idiom does the author use? What does it mean?

_____

_____

> ▶ Reread paragraph 8. Then follow the directions below.

2. What type of figurative language do you find in paragraph 8 and what does it compare?

_____

_____

3. Use a metaphor to describe Twyla.

_____

_____

Name _____

Suffixes –ness, –ment

▶ Complete the chart with words that contain the suffix *–ness* or *–ment*.

–ness	*–ment*

▶ Write a sentence for each word in the chart.

_____

_____

_____

_____

_____

_____

_____

Name _____

Text Structure

Authors organize information in logical ways so readers can understand key ideas. They want readers to notice how ideas fit together. The way authors organize ideas in a text is called its **text structure**.

Authors choose a text structure that suits their purpose. For example, if authors want to tell a story, they organize events in the order that they happened.

Text Structure	Purpose
Compare/Contrast	To explain how things or ideas are alike and different
Cause/Effect	To explain what happened and why
Chronology	To explain events in order
Problem/Solution	To explain how problems were solved

▶ **Reread the "On My Own" section on page 132 in** *Blind Ambition* **and answer the following questions.**

1. What helps Matthew play paintball and help at his school plays?

_____

_____

2. How do these details help you understand the text structure?

_____

_____

▶ **Reread paragraph 4 in** *Blind Ambition*.

3. What is the text structure? How does the text structure help you understand the story?

_____

_____

Name _____

Words with Vowels Sounds /ŭ/, /yōo/, and /ōo/

> Circle the word or words with the short *u* sound in each sentence.

1. What a beautiful bunch of grapes!

2. The mule got stuck in the ditch.

3. A trunk is useful to an elephant.

4. I trust people who tell the truth.

5. Scatter the crumbs for the ducks.

6. The man in the truck was hungry.

7. It is fun to amuse the baby.

8. We played with the puppies for hours.

9. If we are lucky, we'll be home for lunch.

10. Aunt Ruth told me to brush my hair.

Name _____

Critical Vocabulary

You can use the words you learn from reading as you talk and write.

> **Use your understanding of the Critical Vocabulary words to support your answers to the questions below. Then use the Critical Vocabulary words as you talk with a partner about your answers.**

1. What's the difference between a silly situation and an **absurd** situation?

_____

_____

2. What would you do if you witnessed one classmate **taunt** another?

_____

3. Why might someone **forfeit** the chance to win a new bike?

_____

_____

4. What foods have you **despised** in the past but now enjoy eating?

_____

5. What would you do if you think an approaching dog might be **ferocious**?

_____

6. When have you prepared **elaborately** for an event?

_____

7. What would you want if you could have anything you **coveted**?

_____

> **Write a sentence using two Critical Vocabulary words below.**

_____

Name _____

Plot

Most stories include the same main parts, or elements. Story elements include **plot**, the series of events that make up the story. In a plot, the **rising action** builds as readers learn the story's problem. The action reaches a **climax** when the tension in the story is the greatest. In the story's **falling action**, readers learn about the **resolution**, or how the story's problem is solved.

In historical fiction, characters are from another time and place, or **setting**. The characters give readers insight as to how people of that time might have thought, spoken, and acted. Often, events that happen at the time of the story's setting have a great impact on characters' lives.

▶ **Read page 140 in *The Game of Silence* and answer the following question.**

1. What details tell you about the setting? How does the setting add to the story's plot?

   _____

   _____

▶ **Read paragraphs 8–11 in *The Game of Silence* and answer the following questions.**

2. What details show how Omakayas and Pinch get along?

   _____

   _____

3. Why are these details part of the rising action?

   _____

   _____

4. Which events tell the falling action?

   _____

   _____

Name _____

Suffixes –y and -*ly*

> Complete the chart with words that contain the suffix –*y* or –*ly*.

–*y*	–*ly*

> Write a sentence for each word in the chart.

_____

_____

_____

_____

_____

_____

_____

Name _____

Author's Craft

Author's craft is the language and techniques a writer uses to make his or her writing interesting and communicate ideas to the reader. Sometimes authors use **literal language** to express ideas in a text. The chart below shows different techniques authors use to express ideas.

Technique	Definition
Voice	The author's style that makes his or her writing unique
Language	Vocabulary, precise nouns, sensory words, and vivid verbs that make the text more interesting
Hyperbole	Exaggerations that make things sound bigger, better, or more than what they truly are

> **Reread paragraph 14 and answer the following questions.**

1. What phrases does the author use to describe the gathering?

_____

_____

2. How does this language contribute to the author's voice?

_____

_____

_____

3. What purpose does this imagery serve?

_____

_____

_____

Vowel Sounds o͝o and o͞o

▶ **Read each sentence. Find the word that includes the sound of o͝o or o͞o. Underline the letter or group of letters that stand for that sound. Below the sentence, underline the kind of sound you hear in the word.**

1. My favorite kind of food is pizza.

   o͝o   o͞o

2. Does your dad prefer butter or sauce on his noodles?

   o͝o   o͞o

3. Louis is a very talented violin player.

   o͝o   o͞o

4. What a delicious cookie!

   o͝o   o͞o

5. Connor is in a bad mood when he doesn't get enough sleep.

   o͝o   o͞o

6. When Amad went fishing, he put a worm on his hook.

   o͝o   o͞o

7. What kind of books does Sara like to read?

   o͝o   o͞o

8. My bedroom is painted in a lovely purple.

   o͝o   o͞o

9. Erica needs to look in both directions before she crosses the street.

   o͝o   o͞o

10. Hannah knows that she should always try her best.

    o͝o   o͞o

Name _____

Critical Vocabulary

You can use the words you learn from reading as you talk and write.

> **Use your understanding of the Critical Vocabulary words to support your answers to the questions below.**

1. If you could **spare** the money, would you go to an **auction**? Why or why not?

_____

_____

_____

2. If someone handed you a **brimming** glass, what would you do with it?

_____

3. If you were writing a song, what would the **verses** be about? What idea would be repeated in the **chorus**?

_____

_____

4. If you were wandering and someone asked you why you were **drifting**, what would you tell them?

_____

_____

5. If you hung some wet clothes on a line for a few hours on a hot sunny day, would they be **damp** or dry when you came to get them? How do you know?

_____

> **Choose two of the Critical Vocabulary words and use them in a sentence.**

_____

Name _____

Author's Craft

When people talk, they use different kinds of language. Their language depends on what they are doing and who they are with. Authors also use different kinds of language when they write. The chart below explains formal and informal language. These two types of language are used by authors to help readers better understand characters in a story.

	What It Is	Where It Is Used	Example
• **Formal language**	• The way people speak in important situations or with people they don't know well • Complete sentences with standard grammar and vocabulary	• Newspaper articles • Speeches • School reports	*The music was lively and rhythmic.*
• **Informal language**	• The way people speak at relaxed events with family or friends • Sentence fragments, irregular grammar, and slang vocabulary	• At home with family • Conversations with friends	*I sure am lovin' that music!*

▶ **Reread paragraph 1 in *Rent Party Jazz*. Then answer the questions.**

1. What does the word *mah* mean as it is used in this sentence? Is this an example of formal or informal language?

   _____

2. Why do you think the author chose to include this sentence in the story?

   _____

   _____

▶ **Reread page 170 in *Rent Party Jazz*. Then cite examples of formal or informal language.**

3. Formal language: _____

   Informal language: _____

Name _____

Multiple Syllable Words with Vowel Sounds o͝o, o͞o

> Read each sentence. At the end of each sentence is the vowel sound o͝o or o͞o. Find a word from the box that contains this vowel sound and makes sense in the sentence. Write that word in the blank.

o͝o	o͞o
woodwork	caboose
graceful	poodle
octopus	youthful
scrapbook	amuse
pudding	tulips

1. Jessica is excited for spring, when the _____ in her garden will bloom. (o͞o)

2. The _____ dancer seemed to float across the stage. (o͝o)

3. Do you like chocolate _____ ? (o͝o)

4. The train had a red _____ . (o͞o)

5. Many animals live in the ocean, including the whale and the _____ . (o͞o)

6. My friend's dog is a black _____ . (o͞o)

7. I enjoy reading funny books because they _____ me. (o͞o)

8. The _____ was filled with pictures from my mom's childhood. (o͝o)

Name _____

Suffixes –*ful*, –ous, –less

> Complete the chart with other words that contain each suffix.

–*ful*	–*ous*	–*less*
successful	adventurous	lifeless

> Write a short story with words using the three suffixes.

_____

_____

_____

_____

_____

_____

Name _____

Plot

Plot is one of the elements of a story. The plot is a series of events in a story. It usually includes a problem that characters face and the actions they take to solve their problems. Sometimes the plot is impacted by the setting of a story or the cultural background of the characters.

> **Reread pages 171–172 of *Rent Party Jazz* and answer the questions.**

1. What is the setting of the story? How does the setting affect the plot?

_____

_____

_____

2. How does Sonny meet Smilin' Jack? Why is this event important to the plot?

_____

_____

_____

3. Which event was the climax of the plot?

_____

_____

4. What are some other ways the story's setting impacts the plot?

_____

_____

_____

_____

_____

Name _____

Theme

The **theme** is the main message, lesson, or moral of a story. The theme helps readers understand the message that authors want to get across.

> **Reread page 173 in** *Rent Party Jazz*. **Then answer the question.**

1. According to Smilin' Jack, what do the neighbors get in return for their kindness? How does this detail help develop the theme?

_____

_____

_____

> **Review pages 178–180. Then answer the questions.**

2. What is the theme of this selection?

_____

_____

_____

3. Cite evidence from the text that helps you determine the theme.

_____

_____

_____

_____

4. State the theme in your own words.

_____

_____

Vowel Sounds /ou/, /ô/

> **Read the words in the box. Then look at each sentence. Write the word that fits best on the line. Does the word have an /ou/ vowel or an /ô/ vowel? Circle the correct vowel below the sentence.**

/ou/	/ô/
cloud	talk
owl	yawn
frown	draw
crouch	fault
house	salt

1. You may _____ when you are unhappy.
　　　　　　　　/ou/ /ô/

2. Please don't _____ during the movie.
　　　　　　　　/ou/ /ô/

3. Do you like _____ on your french fries?
　　　　　　　　/ou/ /ô/

4. I heard the hoot of the _____ last night.
　　　　　　　　　　　　/ou/ /ô/

5. I really like to _____ pictures of animals.
　　　　　　　　　/ou/ /ô/

6. My _____ is the last one on the left side of the street.
　　　　/ou/ /ô/

7. The fluffy _____ floated across the sky.
　　　　　　　/ou/ /ô/

8. The sleepy baby began to _____ .
　　　　　　　　　　　　/ou/ /ô/

Name _____

Critical Vocabulary

You can use the words you learn from reading as you talk and write.

▶ **Use your understanding of the Critical Vocabulary words to support your answers to the questions below.**

1. Imagine a character saying to the hero in a story: "If you do, you could **perish**." What might the hero be planning to do?

   _____

   _____

   _____

2. When might you be asked to clean up some **debris**? How would you do it?

   _____

   _____

   _____

3. Imagine that there was a movie called "**Surge**." What would it be about?

   _____

   _____

   _____

▶ **Choose two of the Critical Vocabulary words and use them in sentences. Include a synonym and/or an antonym for each vocabulary word you use.**

   _____

   _____

Name _____

Point of View

Point of view is the way authors tell about events. In primary sources, events are told by the people who experienced them. In secondary sources, experiences and events are written by authors who did not experience the events first-hand.

> ▶ **Reread pages 187–188 of** *Hurricanes: A Force of Nature.*

1. Which part of this text is a primary source? Explain.

_____

_____

2. Which part of the text is a secondary source? Explain.

_____

_____

3. What details do you learn in the primary source that are not included in the secondary source?

_____

_____

> ▶ **Reread pages 186 and 190 to compare and contrast the information in primary and secondary sources.**

4. Compare the accounts. What topic do they both tell about?

_____

5. How are the accounts different?

_____

_____

Two-Syllable Words with the Vowel Sounds /ou/ and /ô/

▶ **Read each sentence. Find the word that includes the sound of /ou/ or /ô/. Underline the letter or group of letters that stands for the sound. Below the sentence, underline the kind of sound you hear in the word you underlined.**

1. My dad used the chainsaw to trim the large tree.
   /ou/   /ô/

2. Do you prefer walking or riding in a car?
   /ou/   /ô/

3. The banker put the money into the savings account.
   /ou/   /ô/

4. "I feel lousy!" said Marcus.
   /ou/   /ô/

5. My grandmother makes a delicious clam chowder.
   /ou/   /ô/

6. I made a sandwich because I was hungry.
   /ou/   /ô/

7. I am doubtful that I will be able to attend.
   /ou/   /ô/

8. The princess lived in the highest tower.
   /ou/   /ô/

9. The medicine tasted awful!
   /ou/   /ô/

10. Talking is not permitted in the library.
    /ou/   /ô/

Name _____

Critical Vocabulary

You can use the words you learn from reading as you talk and write.

▶ **Use your understanding of the Critical Vocabulary words to support your answers to the questions below.**

1. How do people behave **adoringly** toward others?

_____

_____

2. In what ways does a person need to be **capable** in order to drive a car?

_____

_____

3. Have you ever been a **spectator** at a big event? Did you enjoy it? Why or why not?

_____

_____

4. What do you regard with **disbelief**? Why?

_____

_____

▶ **Choose two of the Critical Vocabulary words and use them in sentences. Include a synonym and/or an antonym for each vocabulary word you use.**

_____

_____

Name _____

Elements of Drama

A play, sometimes known as a **drama**, is a story that is written to be performed by actors in front of an audience. Dramas have elements that help people perform the story. A **cast of characters** lists each character in the play. The name of each character appears before the words he or she says. These words are called **dialogue**. **Stage settings** tell the audience where and when each scene takes place. **Stage directions** tell the actors what to do and how to speak.

> ▶ **Reread page 201 in *Catch Me If You Can*. Then answer the question.**

1. How do the words and their arrangement on the page look different from other stories or poems?

_____

_____

_____

_____

_____

> ▶ **Reread page 203 in *Catch Me If You Can*. Then answer the questions.**

2. What event is taking place in this part of the play?

_____

3. Which characters are speaking?

_____

4. What do the stage directions tell the spectators to do?

_____

_____

Name _____

Latin Roots vis, aud, spec

▶ Complete the chart with other words that contain each root.

vis	aud	spec
vision	audio	spectrum

▶ Write sentences with words using the three roots.

_____

_____

_____

_____

_____

_____

Name _____

Idioms, Adages, and Proverbs

Idioms, adages, and proverbs are types of common sayings that have meanings beyond what can be understood by their individual words. An **idiom** means something different from what the words say. An **adage** expresses a truth or gives advice. A **proverb** expresses a short truth based on common sense or experience.

▶ **Reread page 200 in** *Catch Me If You Can.* **Then answer the questions.**

1. What adage can you identify? What does this saying mean?

_____

_____

2. What does this saying mean in relation to the text?

_____

_____

▶ **Reread page 202 in** *Catch Me If You Can.* **Then answer the questions.**

3. What proverb or idiom appears in the dialogue of Young John?

_____

4. What does Young John mean?

_____

5. What proverb or idiom does Atalanta say? What does Atalanta mean?

_____

6. How would the meaning of each expression be different if you thought about the meaning of each individual word?

_____

_____

Name _____

Words with Vowel + /r/ Sounds /är/, /âr/, /îr/

▶ **Look at the following story. Notice that many of the sentences have blanks in them. As you read the story, pick a word from the box that makes sense in the blank. Write the word on the line.**

/är/	/âr/	/îr/
large	affair	dreary
art	blare	cheerful
party	scare	tearful
barn	fair	peered

A Birthday Surprise

I woke up in a _____ mood. It was my birthday! I couldn't wait

for my friends to arrive for the _____ . I pulled back the curtain

and _____ out of my window. The sky looked dark and _____ .

I watched as _____ raindrops fell to the ground. It just wasn't _____ !

"Don't worry," said Dad. "We'll move the celebration to the _____ . You

can _____ music and dance. You can make cool _____ projects.

It will be a grand _____ !"

Critical Vocabulary

You can use the words you learn from reading as you talk and write.

▷ **Use your understanding of the Critical Vocabulary words to support your answers to the questions below.**

1. A movie reviewer says, "A new star has **burst** out in this film." What do you think that means?

   _____

   _____

2. What would it mean if you were given **opportunities** to travel to other countries? Why would that be **amazing**?

   _____

   _____

   _____

3. If you could make new **immigration** laws, what would they say?

   _____

   _____

4. The word *refuge* means a "safe, protected place." In what way is this word related to "**refugee**"?

   _____

   _____

▷ **Choose two of the Critical Vocabulary words and use them in a sentence.**

   _____

   _____

Name _____

Literary Elements

Literary elements include characters in a story, the setting, the plot, and the events that happen in the story.

> **Reread paragraphs 14 and 15 of** *My Diary from Here to There*. **Then answer the question.**

1. How do the settings influence the plot?

_____

_____

_____

_____

_____

_____

_____

> **Reread paragraph 21 of** *My Diary from Here to There*. **Then answer the questions.**

2. How do the moves from one house to another impact Amada?

_____

_____

_____

3. How do you think the challenges of such a big move seem to affect Amada's siblings?

_____

_____

Prefixes over-, under-

> Complete the chart with other words that contain each prefix.

over–	under–
overcook	undercover

> Write sentences with words using the two prefixes.

_____

_____

_____

_____

_____

_____

Name _____

Point of View

Point of view is who is telling the story. In the first-person point of view, the narrator is telling the story, using the pronouns *I*, *me*, and *we*. In the third-person point of view, the narrator is outside the story, using the pronouns *he*, *she*, and *they*.

▶ **Reread paragraph 1 of *My Diary from Here to There*. Then answer the questions.**

1. From what point of view is this story being told?

_____

2. Why do you think the author chooses this point of view to tell the story?

_____

_____

▶ **Reread paragraphs 19–20 of *My Diary from Here to There*. Then answer the question.**

3. Whose point of view are we reading when we read the letter from Papá? How do you know?

_____

_____

▶ **Reread paragraphs 32–33 of *My Diary from Here to There*. Then answer the question.**

4. How has Amada's perspective on living in the United States changed from the beginning of the story to the end?

_____

_____

_____

Name _____

Vowel + /r/ and Suffixes –y, –ly

▶ Read each sentence. Decide which word from the word box best completes the sentence and write it in the blank. Circle the letters in the word that make the vowel sound of / är/, /år/, or /ir/. Does the word have a suffix of –y or –ly? Underline it.

prairie	sparkly	dearly	sparingly
dreary	unfairly	teary	scarcely
fearfully	rarely	sleepily	carelessly

1. When John's mother punished him, even though he didn't break the vase,

   she treated him _____ .

2. Pioneers used to travel across the _____ in covered wagons.

3. My older brother is so busy that I _____ see him.

4. The children were scared that there might be a monster in the closet,

   as they _____ opened the closet door.

5. It rained all morning and the clouds made the day dark and _____ .

6. When my sister lost her favorite toy, she was _____ and sad.

7. The princess wore a _____ gown to the ball.

8. A mother _____ loves all of her children.

Author's Craft

Author's craft is the language and techniques a writer uses to make their writing more interesting. Authors may use **figurative language** to describe events and characters. They may also use **literal language** to tell readers what is happening in a story.

▶ **Reread paragraphs 7–9 of *My Diary from Here to There*. Then answer the questions.**

1. What anecdote, or story by a character, is told?

_____

_____

2. Why does the author choose to have Michi tell an anecdote about her family here?

_____

_____

▶ **Reread paragraph 32 of *My Diary from Here to There*. Then answer the questions.**

3. Find examples of how the author's use of language contributes to Amada's perspective.

_____

_____

_____

_____

4. Find an example in the text that shows how the author uses literal language to show her voice and engage readers.

_____

_____

_____

Name _____

More Vowel + /r/ Sounds /ûr/ /ôr/

> Read each sentence. Choose the word that best replaces the underlined word or words in each sentence and write it on the line. Does the word make an /ûr/ or /ôr/ sound? Circle the letters that stand for the sound.

burn	dirty	burst	world	sore
thirsty	current	board	search	course
return	pure	learn	thirteen	early
worn	worse	cure	record	sport

Sentence	Word	Sound
1. Please put the soiled clothes in the washing machine.	_____	/ûr/ /ôr/
2. The librarian says we have to bring back the books in two weeks.	_____	/ûr/ /ôr/
3. Cara's ankle was aching after soccer practice.	_____	/ûr/ /ôr/
4. The whole neighborhood will look for our lost dog.	_____	/ûr/ /ôr/
5. When it gets cold, we will set fire to the logs in our fireplace.	_____	/ûr/ /ôr/
6. Our planet is made up of land and water.	_____	/ûr/ /ôr/
7. Is it fun to discover new things by reading?	_____	/ûr/ /ôr/
8. The hot sun and sand of the Sahara Desert made the explorers desire water.	_____	/ûr/ /ôr/
9. Track and field is my favorite athletic game.	_____	/ûr/ /ôr/
10. Jacob's assignment was to write an up-to-date report on the volcanic eruption.	_____	/ûr/ /ôr/

Critical Vocabulary

You can use the words you learn from reading as you talk and write.

▶ **Use your understanding of the Critical Vocabulary words from *Prince Charming Misplaces His Bride* to help you finish each sentence.**

1. My brother **sulked** in his room because _____

_____

2. When I heard a **foreboding** click, I knew _____

_____

3. I felt my backbone get **rigid** when _____

_____

4. My hair is **disheveled** because _____

_____

5. Our new puppy gets **feisty** when _____

_____

6. What made the event really **elegant** was _____

_____

7. We felt **intimidated** by the other team because _____

_____

8. I **scowled** at my sister because _____

_____

9. The **episode** with forgotten homework taught me _____

_____

10. The audience's **subdued** response showed _____

_____

▶ **Choose two of the Critical Vocabulary words and use them in a sentence.**

_____

_____

Name _____

Point of View

The **point of view** of a story is told using first-person point of view or third-person point of view. When the story is told in first-person point of view, the narrator of the story is a character in the story. Readers only know that character's perspective. Key words such as *I*, *me*, and *we* signal first-person point of view. In third-person point of view, the narrator is not in the story but is outside the story. Key words such as *he*, *she*, *they* and character names signal third-person point of view.

> **Reread paragraph 13 of *Prince Charming Misplaces His Bride* to determine the point of view. Then answer the questions.**

1. What point of view does the author use in paragraph 13?

_____

_____

2. How do you know?

_____

_____

_____

> **Reread page 253 and answer the question below.**

3. How would the story be different if Frederic were the narrator?

_____

_____

_____

_____

_____

More Vowel + /r/ Sounds /ûr/ /ôr/

worth	worn	worse	world	warn

1. Write three words from the box above with the same /r/ sound.

_____   _____   _____

current	course	courage	cure

2. Write two words from the box above that have two syllables.

_____   _____

worthwhile	further	thirteen

3. Write the word from the box above that is a number.

_____

board	sport	world	afford

4. Which words from the word boxes make the same /ôr/ sound as the word *sore*? Write the words on the blanks and circle the letters that stand for the /ôr/ sound.

_____   _____   _____

_____   _____   _____

Name _____

Prefixes sub-, fore-

> Complete the chart with other words that contain each prefix.

sub-	fore-
subtopic	foreground

> Write sentences with words using the two prefixes.

_____

_____

_____

_____

_____

Name _____

Theme

The **theme** of a story is the main message, lesson, or moral of the text. Sometimes the theme is stated by the author. Other times, the theme is implied using details in the text. The reader is left to figure out the theme.

> **Reread page 253 of *Prince Charming Misplaces His Bride* to determine the theme. Then answer the questions below.**

1. What advice does Reginald give Frederic and in what way?

_____

_____

_____

_____

2. What message or lesson is the author trying to communicate?

_____

_____

_____

_____

3. How can you use this message and relate it to your everyday life?

_____

_____

_____

_____

Name _____

Text and Graphic Features

Text and graphic features can present important parts of a story. Different kinds of type such as boldface, italics, or capital letters may be used by an author to communicate something important to get the reader's attention. Visuals such as illustrations, diagrams, and maps help explain ideas in a text.

▶ **Revisit pages 238 and 239 in** *Prince Charming Misplaces His Bride.* **Then answer the question below.**

1. What do you notice about the text on these pages? Why do you think the text is shown in this way?

   _____

   _____

   _____

▶ **Revisit page 245 in** *Prince Charming Misplaces His Bride.* **Then answer the question.**

2. What details in the illustration help you understand the relationship between Ella and Frederic?

   _____

   _____

   _____

▶ **Revisit page 250 in** *Prince Charming Misplaces His Bride.* **Then answer the question.**

3. How does the text change on this page, and why does the author change it?

   _____

   _____

   _____

Regular and Irregular Plurals

▶ **Read each sentence. Decode the underlined nouns. Write the nouns in the plural on the line below.**

1. The child took the book from the shelf.

_____

2. He has curly, red hair.

_____

3. Mary had her tooth pulled.

_____

4. The baby began to play with the toy.

_____

5. The plant attracted the butterfly.

_____

6. The man brought the box into the store.

_____

Name _____

Critical Vocabulary

You can use the words you learn from reading as you talk and write.

▶ **Use your understanding of the Critical Vocabulary words from** *Smokejumpers to the Rescue* **to support your answers to the questions below.**

1. Would you recommend a person who is **timid** work as a smokejumper? Why or why not?

_____

_____

_____

2. What are some strenuous tasks that smokejumpers must perform in their job?

_____

_____

_____

▶ **Write a sentence for each of the Critical Vocabulary words.**

_____

_____

_____

_____

Name _____

Text Structure

The way an author organizes information in a text is called its **text structure**. An author chooses a text structure that highlights the reason for writing.

If the author wants to . . .	the text structure may be . . .
tell events in the order they happened	chronological order
explain what happened and why	cause and effect
show how things are alike and different	compare and contrast

Another text structure is problem-and-solution. The author gives details about a problem and then describes how to solve it or deal with it.

▶ **Revisit *Smokejumpers to the Rescue!* to determine the text structure.**

1. What text structure does the author use?

_____

2. Cite examples that show the text structure.

_____

_____

_____

_____

3. What other text structure did you find? Why did the author use it?

_____

_____

Name _____

Regular and Irregular Plurals

> Match the two parts of the sentences. Draw a line to connect the sentence beginning to the correct sentence ending.

1. One policeman Two policemen	are directing traffic. is directing traffic.
2. My tooth My teeth	is loose. are loose.
3. The cup The cups	are clean. is clean.
4. The man The men	are playing golf. is playing golf.
5. The mouse The mice	are eating cheese. is eating cheese.

> Choose the correct answer. Write the correct answer on the blank.

1. The child's _____ are very small. foots feets feet

2. I saw several _____ in the barn. mouse mice mices

3. The _____ are on the playground. childs childrens children

4. The _____ swam in the lake. geese gooses geeses

Name _____

Critical Vocabulary

You can use the words you learn from reading as you talk and write.

▶ **Use details from *Perseus and the Fall of Medusa* to support your answers to the questions below. Then use the Critical Vocabulary words as you talk with a partner about your answers.**

1. Who **devised** a plan to trick Perseus into killing Medusa? Explain.

_____

2. Why was Danae in **distress** as Perseus left the palace?

_____

3. How would you feel if your parents announced that your family was going on an **odyssey**?

_____

4. Was it Perseus's **destiny** to be killed by Medusa?

_____

5. Would you consider a person to be a **mortal** being? Explain.

_____

▶ **Write a sentence using one of the Critical Vocabulary words below.**

_____

_____

_____

Elements of Drama

A drama, or **play**, is a story that is meant to be performed for an audience. The **script** of a play tells directors, actors, and backstage helpers exactly how to perform the play on stage.

- The **cast of characters** is a list of people, animals, or other beings in the play. It usually appears at the beginning of the script.

- **Stage directions** appear throughout a script and are usually in italic type. Stage directions may describe the setting for each scene, the way a character should say a line, or when characters enter, exit, or move.

- The words characters say to each other are called **dialogue**. Each line of dialogue begins with the name of the character who should say those words. Dialogue builds to reveal the plot of the play.

▶ **Review page 268 of *Perseus and the Fall of Medusa*. Then answer the question.**

1. What information in the Cast of Characters helps you predict what might happen in the play?

   _____

   _____

▶ **Reread lines 9–18 of *Perseus and the Fall of Medusa*. Then answer the questions.**

2. What do the stage directions show about how each character should speak?

   _____

3. How does the dialogue reveal the problem Perseus faces?

   _____

   _____

   _____

Name _____

Suffixes –able, –ible

> Complete the chart with other words that contain each suffix.

–able	–ible

> Write sentences with words using the two suffixes.

_____

_____

_____

_____

_____

_____

Name _____

Figurative Language

Figurative language is the use of words or phrases to suggest more than what the words actually mean. Figurative language may help readers understand an idea by reminding them of a well-known person or thing. It may make comparisons or create strong images. Using figurative language helps readers see ideas in new ways.

Type	What It Is	Example
Allusion	A brief reference to a person, place, thing, or idea from literature or history; many allusions refer to myths	*It was no surprise that a ship named Poseidon sank to the bottom of the sea!*
Simile	The use of the words *like* or *as* to compare one thing to another thing	*The anger in Eugene's eyes burned as bright as coals.*
Imagery	A description that creates a strong image in the reader's mind or appeals to other senses	*The worn wooden door was cracked and splintered.*

▶ **Reread lines 22–35 from *Perseus and the Fall of Medusa* and answer the questions.**

1. What are some examples of imagery in the text? How do they help readers?

_____

_____

2. Which stage direction includes a simile? What does this comparison do?

_____

_____

▶ **Reread page 276 of *Perseus and the Fall of Medusa* to identify the use of figurative language.**

3. The *Odyssey* is a well-known Greek poem about the journey of a hero. What comparison does the author make to this poem?

_____

_____

Spelling Word Sort: Adding -ed or -ing

> Choose three spelling words from the word box that follow each rule. Write them on the lines in the correct boxes.

striped	surprising	dripped	begged
skipped	handled	forgetting	dancing
traced	rising	winning	spinning

Add –ed: drop the final e before adding –ed	_____	_____	_____
Add –ed: double the final consonant before adding –ed	_____	_____	_____
Add –ing: drop the final e before adding –ing	_____	_____	_____
Add –ing: double the final consonant before adding –ing	_____	_____	_____

Name _____

Critical Vocabulary

You can use the words you learn from reading as you talk and write.

▶ Use your understanding of the Critical Vocabulary words to support your answers to the questions below.

1. How would you feel if something made you **furious**?

_____

_____

2. If you go to the movie theater **occasionally**, how often do you go?

_____

_____

3. Where is a place where you might feel **secure**? Explain.

_____

_____

▶ Write a sentence using two Critical Vocabulary words below.

_____

_____

_____

_____

Name _____

Text and Graphic Features

Informational texts often include **text features** such as headings and boldfaced words. Informational texts usually include one or more graphic features such as photographs, maps, and illustrations.

> **Reread page 282 in** *St. Augustine: A Story of America*. **Answer the questions.**

1. How do the headings and timeline add to the meaning of the text?

_____

_____

> **Reread page 284. Then answer the questions below.**

2. What do you learn from looking at the map from 1591? How does it add to the meaning of the text?

_____

_____

> **Look at the photographs and reread the captions on page 289. Then answer the question.**

3. How do the photographs and captions contribute to the meaning of the text?

_____

_____

_____

Suffixes –en, –ic

> Complete the chart with other words that contain each suffix.

–en	–ic

> Write sentences with words using the two suffixes.

_____

_____

_____

_____

_____

_____

Name _____

Text Structure

Information in nonfiction texts can be organized in a number of ways. Identifying the **text structure**, or the way in which the information is organized, can help you better understand a nonfiction text.

▶ **Reread pages 282–283 of** *St. Augustine: A Story of America.* **Then answer the questions.**

1. What is the text structure on these pages? How do you know?

_____

_____

_____

▶ **Reread paragraphs 14–18 and answer the questions.**

2. What was the effect of Robert Searles capturing a Spanish ship? What word signals the text structure?

_____

_____

_____

3. What text structure does the author use for "Building a Strong Fort"?

_____

4. What is the problem? What is the solution?

_____

▶ **Reread paragraphs 25–29 to determine the text structure.**

5. What is the text structure? What clues helped you determine the structure?

_____

Name _____

Recognize Root Words: Suffixes -able, -ible

> Complete the crossword puzzle with words with suffixes *-able* and *-ible*.

Across

4. car with a folding or detachable top

_____

5. difficult to believe, extraordinary

_____

7. a person who is pleasant and

charming _____

8. real; able to be true _____

9. Providing ease and relaxation; free from

pain _____

Down

1. able to be known beforehand

_____

2. very bad; awful

_____

3. inexpensive; reasonably priced

_____

6. something that can't be seen

_____

Name _____

Author's Purpose

Author's purpose is the author's reason for writing. Based on his or her purpose, an author uses language and information in certain ways. Paying attention to this use of language and information can help a reader determine the author's perspective on the topic.

▶ **Reread pages 284–285 in** *St. Augustine: A Story of America*. **Then answer the questions below.**

1. What is the author's purpose for writing this selection?

_____

_____

2. What is the author's perspective toward the topic? Explain.

_____

_____

_____

▶ **Reread pages 292–294. Then answer the questions.**

3. What is the author's perspective about "St. Augustine Today"?

_____

_____

4. What text evidence supports this?

_____

_____

_____

Recognize Root Words

▶ **Read each sentence. Underline the word that has a word ending of either
–ing or *–ed*. Then write the root word on the line provided.**

1. The squirrel buried the nuts in the ground. _____

2. Timothy scraped his knee when he fell off his bike. _____

3. Lillian was so cold, she was shaking! _____

4. Roberto tried to do his best on the test. _____

5. Do you like to go hiking? _____

6. Every week, my family goes shopping for groceries. _____

7. Jermaine scratched the spot where a mosquito bit him. _____

8. Are you good at adding numbers together? _____

9. My puppy is happy to be outside digging in our yard. _____

10. My dad thinks that riding a train to work is very convenient. _____

Name _____

Critical Vocabulary

You can use the words you learn from reading as you talk and write.

▶ **Use your understanding of the Critical Vocabulary words to support your answers to the questions below. Then use the words as you talk with a partner about your answers.**

1. What activity would you perform in a **dignified** manner?

_____

_____

2. What new technology has **stunned** you lately?

_____

_____

3. Why is it important to be a **polished** speaker?

_____

_____

4. If you **regretted** something you had said, what could you do?

_____

_____

5. What comedy actor do you find **hysterical**?

_____

_____

6. How can you tell if a friend is an **observant** person?

_____

_____

Name _____

7. What is the best way to **flatter** you?

_____

_____

8. What would you do if your homework was **trampled**?

_____

_____

> Write a sentence using two Critical Vocabulary words below.

_____

_____

Name _____

Ideas and Support

When authors present their **ideas** in a nonfiction text, they must have **support**, or be backed up by reasons and evidence. Authors may have a **perspective**, or attitude about the topic of the text. A text can have different kinds of reasons and evidence.

- A **fact** is a statement that is true and can be proved. Authors also provide details and examples to prove their point.
- An **opinion** tells what someone feels or believes is true. It cannot be proved, but reasons or evidence provided with an opinion may make it seem true.

▶ **Reread paragraphs 17 and 18 in** *The Beatles Were Fab (and They Were Funny)* **and answer the question below.**

1. How do the authors support their perspective that the Beatles were funny?

_____

_____

_____

_____

▶ **Reread paragraphs 23 and 24 and answer the question below.**

2. What is the authors' opinion about how the Beatles behaved once they were famous? What supports this idea?

_____

_____

_____

_____

Name _____

Recognize Root Words in Multisyllabic Words

▶ **Read each sentence. Write the root word of the underlined word on the line.**

1. The football team is <u>undefeated</u> this season. _____

2. We <u>repainted</u> my room a bright blue. _____

3. His grades are <u>improving</u> because he has been working hard. _____

4. My favorite magic trick is the <u>disappearing</u> coin. _____

5. My mom <u>disinfected</u> my cut before putting on the bandage. _____

6. My grandmother <u>subscribed</u> to her favorite magazine for an entire year. _____

7. I found the movie about airplanes to be quite <u>uninteresting</u>. _____

8. I am <u>rethinking</u> my decision to go to the park with my friends. _____

Name _____

Suffixes –ity, –ty

A **suffix** is a word part added to the end of a base word that changes the meaning of the word. When the suffixes **–ity** and **–ty** are placed at the end of a base word, its part of speech changes.

> Complete the chart with words that contain suffixes –ity and –ty.

–ity	–ty

> Choose 3 words from the chart and write a sentence for each word.

_____

_____

_____

_____

_____

_____

_____

Name _____

Text Structure

Text structure is how authors organize their texts. Sometimes a selection has more than one text structure. In selections with multiple types of text structures, the authors organize parts of their texts based on what will best get their ideas across.

Text Structures	Purpose
Comparison/Contrast	To tell how ideas or topics are alike and different
Chronological	To tell events in order of how they happened
Problem/Solution	To explain a problem and tell how it is solved

▶ Reread paragraphs 10–13 to analyze *The Beatles Were Fab (and They Were Funny)* for its structure. Then answer the questions.

1. How is this part of the text organized?

_____

2. What clues do the authors include to show the text structure?

_____

_____

3. How does knowing the text's structure help you understand the author's purpose?

_____

_____

▶ Reread paragraphs 15–17. Then answer the question.

4. How do these paragraphs show the passage of time?

_____

_____

_____

_____

Name _____

Figurative Language

Authors use **figurative language**, such as **idioms,** express events and ideas in a way that is different from their literal meanings. Authors may also use **descriptive language** and **sensory words** to appeal to readers' senses. These vivid details help readers picture what is happening in the text.

> **Reread paragraph 5 in *The Beatles Were Fab*. Answer the question below.**

1. How do the authors use figurative language in this paragraph? Explain.

_____

_____

_____

_____

> **Reread paragraph 26. Then answer the questions.**

2. What figurative language do the authors use to describe Beatlemania during the 1964 tour?

_____

_____

3. What imagery helps you imagine the places the Beatles performed?

_____

_____

> **Reread paragraphs 49–50 and answer the question.**

4. What examples of descriptive and sensory words do the authors use to help you visualize the Beatles' arrival at Shea Stadium?

_____

Name _____

Final Long e

▶ **Read each sentence. Underline the word that has a final long _e_ sound. Then circle the letter or letters that stand for that sound.**

1. My teacher put a smiley face sticker on my book report.

2. The wooden doors in the old house are squeaky.

3. My favorite breed of dog is a collie.

4. Do you like the sound of a canary singing?

5. Charlie plays many sports and is a talented athlete.

6. My grandmother makes a delicious beef and barley soup.

7. The food was so spicy that it made my eyes water!

8. It is important to eat healthy foods like fruits and vegetables.

9. The apple pie had a flaky crust.

10. This book is about a pixie who lives in an enchanted forest.

Critical Vocabulary

You can use the words you learn from reading as you talk and write.

> **Use your understanding of the Critical Vocabulary words to support your answers to the questions below. Then use the words as you talk with a partner about your answers.**

1. What might a **curator** at a history museum do?

_____

_____

2. When you take a picture, do you focus on the object in the **foreground** or the **background**? Explain.

_____

_____

> **Write a sentence using at least two of the Critical Vocabulary words below.**

_____

_____

_____

_____

_____

Name _____

Central Idea

Videos, like text selections, can also have a **central idea**. The central idea is what the video is about. Relevant details can be found throughout the video that support the central idea. A central idea and details can be found in what the speakers say and in the images in the video.

▶ Have students answer the following questions about the video.

1. What video clues tell you the central idea of this video?

_____

_____

_____

_____

2. What do you think is the central idea of this video? How can you tell?

_____

_____

_____

_____

3. What relevant details, facts, or evidence support the central idea?

_____

_____

_____

_____

Name _____

Final Long e in Multisyllabic Words

▶ **Read the words in the box. Then read each sentence. Find a word in the box that makes the most sense in the sentence. Write the word on the line and underline the letters that stand for the long *e* sound. Use each word one time. Some words will not be used.**

unhappy	varsity
birdie	parsley
activity	auntie
abbey	Academy
baggie	ability

1. When I was packing my lunch, I put the sandwich in a _____ .

2. My brother was very excited when he made the _____ team.

3. Her _____ to play the guitar is amazing.

4. My mom added _____ to the chicken soup.

5. Jose's _____ lives in the state of Montana.

6. When Lola lost her favorite book, she was very _____ .

7. My older brother and sister go to school at Lane _____ .

8. Physical _____ is important for living a healthy life.

Name _____

Critical Vocabulary

You can use the words you learn from reading as you talk and write.

▶ **Use your understanding of the Critical Vocabulary words to support your answers to the questions below. Then use the words as you talk with a partner about your answers.**

1. Which musician in a marching band provides the **rhythmic** beat?

_____

_____

2. Who do you know that has a **distinctive** voice?

_____

_____

3. What characteristic would you **highlight** as an example of your personality?

_____

_____

4. Do you think elevators will ever be **horizontal**?

_____

_____

▶ **Write a sentence using two Critical Vocabulary words below.**

_____

_____

Name _____

Text Structure

The way a text is organized helps you understand how an author's ideas are connected to one another. Authors use an organization, or **text structure**, that best highlights or emphasizes their central idea.

An author may begin with a familiar idea, and then tell how other ideas are alike and different. This organization is a **compare-and-contrast** text structure. Other text structures include **cause-and-effect** and **problem-solution**.

▶ **Reread paragraph 6 in** *Let's Dance Around the World*. **Then answer the following questions.**

1. What text structure does the author use in this part of the text? Why?

_____

_____

2. How are tap and break dancing alike? How do they differ from folk dancing?

_____

_____

_____

▶ **Reread paragraphs 11–12 and then answer the following questions.**

3. How are the limbo and the Brazilian capoeira different from one another? How are they similar?

_____

_____

_____

_____

Name _____

Suffixes –er, –or, –ist

When you see a word with the suffix *–er*, *–or*, and *–ist*, look for a base word as a clue to the meaning of the word. The words *sail**or***, *hunt**er***, and *typ**ist*** are made up of a base word and a suffix.

▶ **Complete the chart with other words that contain the suffixes *–er*, *–or*, and *–ist*. (Hint: think of job titles to help you come up with words.)**

–er	–or	–ist

▶ **Choose 3 words from the chart and write a sentence for each word.**

_____

_____

_____

_____

_____

_____

_____

Text and Graphic Features

Informational texts often include **visuals**, such as charts, diagrams, photographs, and illustrations. Pictures and other kinds of visuals add to a reader's understanding of a written text. They present new information that may be hard to explain using just words. Labeled photographs or illustrations can show important details that make the meaning of a text clearer.

▶ **Reread paragraph 5 in *Let's Dance Around the World*. Then answer the following questions.**

1. How does the photograph connect to the text?

_____

_____

2. Why do you think the authors include the photograph of the break dancer?

_____

_____

▶ **Reread page 343 and answer the following questions.**

3. What text or graphic features are shown on this page?

_____

_____

4. What new information do you learn from the photos that is not in the text?

_____

_____

Recognize Root Words

▶ **Read each sentence. Underline the word that has a word ending of -*er*, -*est*, -*ed*, or -*es* added to a root word. Then write the root word on the line provided.**

1. We picked the fluffiest kitten in the litter. _____

2. Do you like to eat fried chicken? _____

3. The daisies look delightful! _____

4. Today is windier than yesterday. _____

5. A good student always tries his or her best. _____

6. My uncle carried the heaviest box. _____

7. We enjoyed riding the ponies at the fair. _____

8. My grandparents have been married for 50 years. _____

9. What kind of stories do you like to read? _____

10. She is much happier when she gets a good night's sleep. _____

Critical Vocabulary

You can use the words you learn from reading as you talk and write.

▶ **Use your understanding of the Critical Vocabulary words to support your answers to the questions below. Then use the words as you talk with a partner about your answers.**

1. How much homework is **necessary** for a fourth grader?

_____

_____

2. What kind of jacket gives you **unsurpassed** protection in a snowstorm?

_____

_____

3. What might a toddler do to cause a **stir** in a supermarket?

_____

4. What is an **extraordinarily** good book you might recommend?

_____

5. What's the best thing about **cruising** on a boat?

_____

6. What happens to the surface of a lake when something heavy **plunges** into it?

_____

▶ **Write a sentence using two Critical Vocabulary words below.**

_____

_____

Elements of Poetry

Poets use sounds, rhythms, and images to create their poems.

Element	What It Is
Rhythm	The flow of words or pattern of beats
Rhyme	Words that have the same ending sounds, such as *snore* and *floor*
Alliteration	The repetition of a beginning letter sound: *five furry foxes*
Onomatopoeia	Words that sound like their meaning, such as *buzz* and *honk*
Imagery	Details that help readers create a mental picture

> **Reread page 351 in *The Art of Poetry* and answer the question below.**

1. What type of poem is this? How does the poem's structure add to its meaning?

_____

_____

> **Reread page 352 in *The Art of Poetry* and answer the questions below.**

2. Who is the speaker addressing?

_____

3. Which phrase is an example of alliteration?

_____

_____

4. Find an example of the author's use of rhyme throughout the poem. How does the rhyme create meaning?

_____

_____

Name _____

Prefixes un– and in–

The prefix **un–** means "not" or "to remove." The prefix **in–** means "not," "without," or "into." A prefix changes the meaning of a base word.

> Complete the chart with words that contain prefixes *un–* and *in–*.

un–	*in–*

> Choose 3 words from the chart and write a sentence for each word.

_____

_____

_____

_____

_____

_____

_____

_____

_____

_____

_____

Name _____

Figurative Language

Poets use phrases called **figurative language** to make their writing more interesting and to help readers imagine what they are reading.

- A **metaphor** compares two things that are alike in some way. Metaphors state that one thing is something else. Example: *Our classroom is a beehive.*
- A **simile** compares two different things using the words *like* or *as*. Example: *The wrestler was as strong as an ox.*
- An **allusion** is a reference to a well-known person, place, event, or form of art. Example: *He used his Herculean strength to lift the fallen tree.*

▶ **Reread page 351 in *The Art of Poetry* and answer the question below.**

1. What kind of figurative language does J. Patrick Lewis use? Explain its meaning.

_____

_____

_____

▶ **Revisit pages 354–355 in *The Art of Poetry* and answer the questions below.**

2. Which famous movie character is referred to in the poem? What does the allusion help you understand?

_____

_____

▶ **Reread page 360 in *The Art of Poetry* and answer the questions below.**

3. What examples of figurative language do you find in the poem?

_____

4. What comparison is being made? Explain.

_____

Name _____

Recognize Root Words in Multisyllabic Words

> **>** **Read each sentence. Write the root word of the underlined word on the line provided.**

1. It is important to have <u>studied</u> for the test. _____

2. The <u>tiniest</u> birds can fly thousands of miles. _____

3. My parents go to many <u>countries</u> together. _____

4. Mason is <u>friendlier</u> than Noah. _____

5. This cartoon is the <u>funniest</u> of all. _____

6. That class is <u>noisier</u> than the one across the hall. _____

7. It is <u>breezier</u> today than it was yesterday. _____

8. The <u>harmonies</u> played by the different instruments were lovely. _____

Theme

The **theme** of a poem is its main message or lesson. Both poets and authors of fictional texts often include themes in their writing. The theme of a poem may be stated, but often the theme is implied by the details the poet uses.

▶ **Reread pages 351–355 in *The Art of Poetry* and answer the question below.**

1. What is the theme of the first three poems in this selection?

_____

_____

_____

_____

▶ **Reread pages 358–359 in *The Art of Poetry* and answer the questions below.**

2. What is the theme of the poem?

_____

3. What message is the poet trying to send to the reader?

_____

_____

_____

▶ **Reread pages 358–360 in *The Art of Poetry* and answer the questions below.**

4. What common themes do you find in the poems written by Francisco X. Alarcón? What is his message to the reader?

_____

_____

Words with /k/, /ng/, and /kw/

▶ **Read each sentence. Find the word that includes a /k/, /kw/, or /ng/ sound. Underline the letter or group of letters that stand for that sound. After the sentence, underline "/k/ Sound", "/kw/ Sound", or "/ng/ Sound".**

1. My brother is younger than me.
   /k/ Sound   /kw/ Sound   /ng/ Sound

2. After spending the day at the beach, Jessie's face was dotted with freckles.
   /k/ Sound   /kw/ Sound   /ng/ Sound

3. Louis is very athletic, and he plays many different sports.
   /k/ Sound   /kw/ Sound   /ng/ Sound

4. Maria goes to the library frequently because she loves to read.
   /k/ Sound   /kw/ Sound   /ng/ Sound

5. What do you wear when you go outside on a brisk day?
   /k/ Sound   /kw/ Sound   /ng/ Sound

6. Elizabeth squealed with delight when she saw the gift inside the box.
   /k/ Sound   /kw/ Sound   /ng/ Sound

7. The little duckling waddled behind its mother on the way to the pond.
   /k/ Sound   /kw/ Sound   /ng/ Sound

8. As she got into bed, Sandra wrapped the fuzzy blanket around her.
   /k/ Sound   /kw/ Sound   /ng/ Sound

9. Fire fighters are heroes because they risk their lives to save people who are in danger.
   /k/ Sound   /kw/ Sound   /ng/ Sound

10. When we traveled through the mountains last summer, I enjoyed the scenic view.
    /k/ Sound   /kw/ Sound   /ng/ Sound

Critical Vocabulary

▶ Use your understanding of the Critical Vocabulary words from *The Mariana Trench* to support your answers to the questions below.

1. Why is the **summit** of Mount Everest famous?

_____

_____

2. What is something **vital** to the exploration of the ocean floor?

_____

_____

3. Why is a **submersible** vehicle useful to oceanographers?

_____

_____

4. What might you have seen in **prehistoric** times?

_____

_____

5. Where might you see a **trench**?

_____

_____

6. What are some things that are needed for living things to **thrive**?

_____

_____

Name _____

7. How could a **remotely**-controlled vehicle help scientists explore the ocean?

_____

_____

8. How could you get a **glimpse** of deep sea creatures?

_____

_____

9. Would you drive an **autonomous** ocean vehicle? Why or why not?

_____

_____

▶ **Choose two of the Critical Vocabulary words and use them in a sentence.**

_____

_____

Central Idea

Sometimes the author tells readers the **central idea** in a sentence. Most often, readers have to figure out the central idea. To determine the central idea, evaluate the relevant details the author includes by asking, "Does this detail tell more about the central idea?"

▶ **Read page 25 in *Mariana Trench*. Then answer the questions below.**

1. What is the central idea of the text on page 25?

_____

2. Evaluate and give two relevant details that support the central idea.

_____

_____

_____

▶ **Choose another section in *Mariana Trench*. Tell the central idea for that section. List at least two supporting details.**

_____

_____

_____

_____

_____

_____

_____

Name _____

Multisyllabic Words with /k/, /ng/, and /kw/

> Read each sentence. Find the word that includes a /k/, /kw/, or /ng/ sound. Underline the letter or group of letters that stand for that sound. After the sentence, underline "/k/ Sound", "/kw/ Sound", or "/ng/ Sound". Also, divide the word into syllables.

1. I felt frantic when I realized that I had forgotten my homework.

      /k/ Sound   /kw/ Sound   /ng/ Sound

2. A donkey was once a common form of travel.

      /k/ Sound   /kw/ Sound   /ng/ Sound

3. Amy did a backward flip off of the diving board.

      /k/ Sound   /kw/ Sound   /ng/ Sound

4. I had a terrible backache after sleeping on the floor of the tent.

      /k/ Sound   /kw/ Sound   /ng/ Sound

5. What is the dog barking at?

      /k/ Sound   /kw/ Sound   /ng/ Sound

6. Diego used the squirt gun to surprise his sister.

      /k/ Sound   /kw/ Sound   /ng/ Sound

7. My little sister is very cranky when she doesn't get a good night's sleep.

      /k/ Sound   /kw/ Sound   /ng/ Sound

8. Many old cars can be found in a junkyard.

      /k/ Sound   /kw/ Sound   /ng/ Sound

9. As I was looking up into the sky, I saw a beautiful rainbow!

      /k/ Sound   /kw/ Sound   /ng/ Sound

10. The equator is the imaginary line that goes around the center of Earth.

      /k/ Sound   /kw/ Sound   /ng/ Sound

Name _____

Greek Roots auto, bio, photo, graph

> Complete the chart with other words that contain the roots *auto, bio, photo,* and *graph*.

auto	bio	photo	graph

> Write a sentence for each word in the chart.

_____

_____

_____

_____

_____

_____

_____

_____

_____

_____

_____

_____

Name _____

Text Structure

The way information is arranged in a text is its **structure**. In a **chronological** text structure, events are told in the order they happen. A **problem-solution** structure describes a problem and how it is solved. A text with a **cause-effect** structure explains what happens and why. In a **comparison** text structure, authors tell how things are alike and different.

> Read paragraphs 17–18 in *Mariana Trench,* and analyze the text structure. Read and answer the questions. Support your answers.

1. What is the structure of this part of the text? How do you know?

_____

_____

_____

_____

2. Why do you think the author uses this text structure?

_____

_____

3. What signal words helped you determine the text structure?

_____

> Reread paragraph 21. Then answer the question.

4. What is the structure of this part of the text? Explain.

_____

_____

_____

Name _____

Text and Graphic Features

Text features help the reader attend to important details in a text. Sometimes authors use **boldface** or *italic* type to point out special or important words. Authors may also use pronunciation guides to help readers figure out how to pronounce difficult words or names of unfamiliar places.

Graphic features, such as photographs and maps, give the reader additional information about a topic.

> **Read pages 18–19 in *Mariana Trench*. Connect the text to the map. Then read and answer the question.**

1. How does the map help you understand more about the text? Explain.

_____

_____

_____

> **Read paragraph 14 on page 25. Then read and answer the question. Support your answer.**

2. Why do you think the author adds the pronunciation guide for the word *Trieste*?

_____

_____

_____

3. Choose another graphic feature. Explain what it shows and why it is included.

_____

_____

_____

Name _____

Words with Final /j/ and /s/

> Read each sentence. Find the word that includes the final sound of /j/ or /s/. Underline the letter or group of letters that stand for that sound. Below the sentence, underline "Final /j/ Sound" or "Final /s/ Sound". Then, write the number of syllables in the word on the line.

1. My mom likes to shop when items are on clearance.
   Final /j/   Final /s/   # of Syllables _____

2. I tried to convince my parents to let me go to the party.
   Final /j/   Final /s/   # of Syllables _____

3. A cold beverage is refreshing on a hot day.
   Final /j/   Final /s/   # of Syllables _____

4. The audience applauded at the end of the concert.
   Final /j/   Final /s/   # of Syllables _____

5. "Who ate all of my porridge?" Baby Bear asked.
   Final /j/   Final /s/   # of Syllables _____

6. What language do you speak?
   Final /j/   Final /s/   # of Syllables _____

7. As I climbed over the fence, I ripped my pants!
   Final /j/   Final /s/   # of Syllables _____

8. After playing outside, Leo had a smudge of dirt on his face.
   Final /j/   Final /s/   # of Syllables _____

9. Marathon runners have to train to run such a long distance.
   Final /j/   Final /s/   # of Syllables _____

10. Police officers and fire fighters need courage to help people in danger.
   Final /j/   Final /s/   # of Syllables _____

Name _____

Critical Vocabulary

You can use the words you learn from reading as you talk and write.

▶ **Use your understanding of the Critical Vocabulary words from *Weird and Wondrous Rocks* to support your answers to the questions below. Then talk with a partner about your answers, using the Critical Vocabulary Words.**

1. Would you describe a fire that went out permanently as an **eternal** flame? Explain.

_____

_____

2. What is the **organic** matter that is keeping the eternal flame burning?

_____

_____

3. Must you travel to an exotic location to find something that is **intriguing**? Explain.

_____

_____

▶ **Use each of the Critical Vocabulary words in a sentence.**

_____

_____

_____

_____

_____

_____

Name _____

Text Structure

The way an author organizes information in a piece of writing is called **text structure**. An author may use a **cause-and-effect** text structure to explain why something happens. The **cause** is the reason something happens. The thing that happens is the **effect**.

> ► Read page 37 in *Weird and Wondrous Rocks*. Then answer the questions.

1. What are two causes for the ringing in the rocks?

_____

_____

_____

2. What is the author's purpose in using cause and effect here?

_____

_____

> ► Read page 40 and answer the questions.

3. What mystery did scientists want to solve in Death Valley National Park?

_____

4. What text structure does the author use to organize information about the mystery?

_____

5. What did the scientists do to solve the mystery?

_____

_____

6. What causes the rocks to move?

_____

_____

Name _____

Words with Final /j/ and /s/

> **Read each sentence. Find the word that includes the final sound of /j/ or /s/. Underline the letter or group of letters that stand for that sound. After the sentence, underline "Final /j/ Sound" or "Final /s/ Sound". Then, write the number of syllables in the word.**

1. The Pilgrims spent a lot of time preparing for their voyage.
   Final /j/   Final /s/   # of Syllables _____

2. It is important to turn off lights to reduce the use of electricity.
   Final /j/   Final /s/   # of Syllables _____

3. Joshua saved his allowance for six months to buy the bicycle.
   Final /j/   Final /s/   # of Syllables _____

4. Solving the multiplication problem was a big challenge for Alex.
   Final /j/   Final /s/   # of Syllables _____

5. Were you able to find a good reference for your report?
   Final /j/   Final /s/   # of Syllables _____

6. The nurse placed a bandage on my arm after I hurt myself.
   Final /j/   Final /s/   # of Syllables _____

7. What an amazing ballet performance!
   Final /j/   Final /s/   # of Syllables _____

8. My mom likes to use a lot of spice in her cooking.
   Final /j/   Final /s/   # of Syllables _____

9. "What a strange little robot!" the princess exclaimed.
   Final /j/   Final /s/   # of Syllables _____

10. I heard the sirens of the ambulance as it rushed to the hospital.
    Final /j/   Final /s/   # of Syllables _____

Name _____

Critical Vocabulary

You can use the words you learn from reading as you talk and write.

> **Use your understanding of the Critical Vocabulary words to support your answers to the questions below. Then talk with a partner about your answers, using the Critical Vocabulary words.**

1. Why is it challenging to explore the **core** of the Mariana Trench? Explain.

_____

_____

2. How might the wind's **wrath** cause a **collision** during a thunderstorm?

_____

_____

3. If a person had many **diverse** activities to choose from, would that person be **idle**? Why or why not?

_____

_____

4. Why is it difficult to **fathom** the size of the universe?

_____

> **Choose two of the Critical Vocabulary words and use them in a sentence.**

_____

_____

_____

_____

Name _____

Author's Craft

Author's craft is the techniques an author uses to make his or her writing unique. **Word choice** reveals the author's attitude, or perspective about a topic. In poetry, readers learn the poet's perspective through his or her use of **figurative language** and **imagery**.

▸ **Read the poem "The Great Barrier Reef" on page 49. Then answer the question.**

1. What is the poet's perspective about the Great Barrier Reef? Cite evidence from the poem to show how his word choice conveys his attitude.

   _____

   _____

▸ **Read the poem "Mount Everest" on page 51. Then answer the question.**

2. What senses does the poet appeal to in "Mount Everest"?

   _____

   _____

3. Write a few sentences or a poem about a place you have visited. Use figurative language and imagery to show your attitude about that place.

   _____

   _____

   _____

   _____

Name _____

Suffixes –ness, –ment

The suffixes *–ness* and *–ment* can be added to base words to change the meaning of the word.

| fair | lovely | enjoy | replace |

▸ **Complete the chart by choosing a word from the box above and adding either** *–ness* **or** *–ment* **to create new words.**

–ness	–ment

▸ **Write a sentence for each word in the chart.**

_____

_____

_____

_____

_____

_____

_____

_____

_____

Name _____

Elements of Poetry

Poems are usually arranged in lines that form stanzas. A **stanza**, or verse, is a group of **lines** in a poem that go together. Like a paragraph, a stanza often tells about one important idea.

Poems have a unique way of describing things. Personification is one of these ways. When a human quality is given to an animal or object, this is called **personification**.

▶ **Read "The Mariana Trench" on page 50 in *Nature's Wonders*. Then answer the questions.**

1. How many stanzas are there in the poem? Which stanza contains personification? What acts as humans do?

   _____

   _____

▶ **Read "Mount Everest" on page 51 in *Nature's Wonders*. Then answer the questions.**

2. What is the subject of the poem?

   _____

3. What is the structure of the poem?

   _____

   _____

4. How does the poem's structure help you understand it?

   _____

   _____

Name _____

Prefixes *re-*, *un-*, and *dis-* in multisyllabic words

▶ Read each sentence. Choose a word from the word box to complete each sentence. Write the word on the line. After writing the word, circle the prefix.

re–	un–	dis–
recreate	unpack	discomfort
refasten	uncommon	dislike
recover	unexpected	disagree

1. Jenna couldn't wait to _____ her suitcase after her vacation.

2. My mom used a needle and thread to _____ the button.

3. I _____ the taste of broccoli.

4. Caleb used the key to _____ the door.

5. The artist tried to _____ the beauty of the sunset in his painting.

6. Becca will sleep until noon on the weekend to _____ from a busy week.

7. Malik felt a lot of _____ after he fell off his bike.

8. Lila looked at the _____ present with excitement.

Critical Vocabulary

You can use the words you learn from reading as you talk and write.

▶ **Use your understanding of the Critical Vocabulary words to answer the questions below. Then talk with a partner about your answers, using the Critical Vocabulary words.**

1. If you saw something that **shattered**, what would it look like?

_____

2. How would you describe a mountain that is **eroding**?

_____

3. How would **sentries** at an important building behave?

_____

4. How would you feel if you stood before a **chasm**?

_____

5. Think of something that **glistens**. How does it look?

_____

6. What would happen if you tried to move an object that was **embedded** in rock? Explain.

_____

▶ **Choose two of the Critical Vocabulary words and use each in a sentence.**

_____

_____

Name _____

Ideas and Support

Some authors write to explain or describe something. Others want to convince you of something.

Authors **support**, or back up, their claims with reasons and evidence. Authors use different kinds of reasons and evidence, such as the following:

- **Facts** are statements that are true and can be proved.

- **Opinions** tell what someone feels or believes. Opinions cannot be proved.

- **Examples** are people, things, or events that show the author's point.

▶ **Read pages 61–62 in** *Grand Canyon: A Trail Through Time* **and answer the questions.**

1. How does the author use evidence to support the ideas presented about the Havasupai Indians?

_____

_____

_____

2. What reasons and evidence support the claim that the layers of rock on the trail have been around for millions of years?

_____

_____

_____

3. Write a sentence that states a fact. Then write a sentence that states an opinion.

_____

_____

Name _____

Prefix inter–

The prefix *inter–* means "between" or "among."

▶ Complete the web with words that contain the prefix *inter–*.

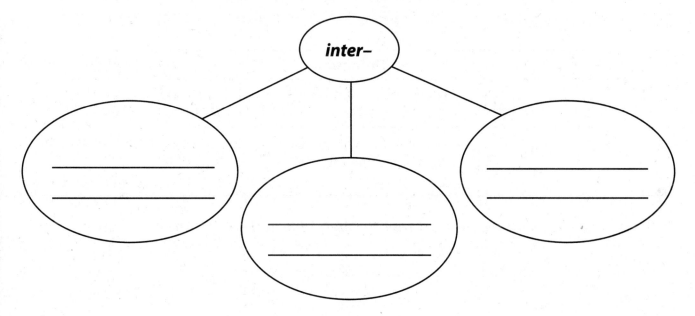

▶ Write a sentence for each word in the web.

_____

_____

_____

_____

_____

_____

_____

_____

Name _____

Simile and Metaphor

Authors describe places or events so that readers can create images in their minds. The images can contribute to the meaning of the text. Often descriptions compare one thing to something else that readers are familiar with. **Similes** and **metaphors** are kinds of comparisons.

	Definition	Example
simile	a comparison that uses the word *like* or *as*	• stood <u>like</u> a statue • <u>as</u> hot <u>as</u> a furnace
metaphor	a comparison without *like* or *as*; may say one thing is something else	• wrapped in a blanket of sunshine • slithering snakes of seaweed

▶ **Read page 61 in *Grand Canyon: A Trail Through Time* and answer the question.**

1. Identify an example of a simile on page 61. What comparison does the author make?

   _____

   _____

   _____

2. Write an example of a simile you might use to describe something about the Grand Canyon.

   _____

   _____

   _____

3. Write an example of a metaphor you might use to describe something about the Grand Canyon.

   _____

   _____

Name _____

Prefixes re-, un-, and dis- in multisyllabic words

▶ Read each sentence. Find the word that includes a prefix of *re-, un-,* or *dis-,* and underline it. After each sentence, circle the kind of prefix you see in the word you underlined.

1. Luke's baseball team was undefeated throughout the whole season.

    re-   un-   dis-

2. Latisha felt terrible about the disagreement with her best friend.

    re-   un-   dis-

3. Ramone felt very unsure on his first day of school.

    re-   un-   dis-

4. I had to rewrite my book report so it wouldn't have any mistakes.

    re-   un-   dis-

5. The school nurse used soap and water to disinfect the cut on my elbow.

    re-   un-   dis-

6. We stopped at a gas station on the highway to refuel the car.

    re-   un-   dis-

7. My mom put the leftover meat into the oven to reheat it for dinner.

    re-   un-   dis-

8. My dad decided to discontinue our membership to the zoo.

    re-   un-   dis-

9. Manuel is confident and unafraid in new situations.

    re-   un-   dis-

10. Alyssa had to remake the brownies for the bake sale because we ate the first batch.

    re-   un-   dis-

Name _____

Author's Craft

Remind students that when authors use descriptive language, they are trying to appeal to the readers' senses. Authors may also use vivid details to help readers picture what is happening and add meaning to the text.

> **Read pages 59–60 of *Grand Canyon* and answer the questions.**

1. On page 59, how does the author use descriptive language to help you picture the Grand Canyon?

   _____

   _____

   _____

   _____

2. In paragraph 5, how does the author help you visualize what is happening in the text?

   _____

   _____

   _____

   _____

   _____

   _____

> **Read paragraph 10 on page 63 and answer the question.**

3. What words does the author use that help you see how lizards act in the Canyon?

   _____

   _____

   _____

Name _____

Suffixes –ful, –less, –ness, –ment

▶ **Read each sentence. Choose a word from the word box that correctly completes each sentence. Write the word on the line.**

–ful	–less	–ness	–ment
wasteful	spotless	weakness	treatment
truthful	endless	dampness	enjoyment
cheerful	flawless	closeness	pavement

1. The house was _____ after we cleaned it.

2. The little boy skinned his knee on the _____ .

3. Grandmother is always _____ when we visit.

4. The _____ of the air made me shiver.

5. The train seemed _____ as we waited for it to pass.

6. When we recycle things we have used, we are not _____ .

7. The children got _____ from visiting the zoo.

8. The _____ of his mother comforted the crying baby.

Name _____

Critical Vocabulary

You can use the words you learn from reading as you talk and write.

▶ **Use your understanding of the Critical Vocabulary words from *Thunder Rose* to support your answers to the questions below.**

1. What could you do to show that you are **partial** to something?

_____

_____

2. How does Tater's **disposition** change when Rose hums her tune?

_____

_____

3. What things might an Olympic athlete **vividly recall**?

_____

_____

4. What actions show that Rose is **resourceful**?

_____

_____

5. What did Rose do that **accentuated** her capture of Jesse Baines and his gang?

_____

_____

6. What kind of thing have you seen that you would call **commendable**?

_____

_____

7. What types of things can cause **devastation**?

_____

_____

8. What places or things might display **splendor**? Explain.

_____

_____

▶ **Choose two of the Critical Vocabulary words and use them in a sentence.**

_____

Name _____

Figurative Language

Authors use **figurative language** to achieve specific purposes, such as to appeal to the senses and add meaning to the text.

> ▶ **Reread paragraphs 8–9 of** *Thunder Rose* **and answer the questions.**

1. What does the phrase "rattling the rafters" mean?

_____

_____

2. What kind of figurative language is this? Why?

_____

3. How does the author's use of exaggeration add meaning to the story?

_____

_____

4. What simile does the author use?

_____

5. Why is this comparison a good choice to describe Rose?

_____

_____

> ▶ **Reread paragraph 11 of** *Thunder Rose.*

6. What sensory words does the author use to describe where Rose lives? To which senses do these words appeal?

_____

Name _____

Suffixes *-ful, -less, -ness, -ment*

▶ **Read the clue. Choose a word from the word box below and combine it with the suffix *-ful, -less, -ness*, or *-ment* to fit the clue.**

peace	rest	weak	pave
color	move	use	neat

1. Unable to stay at rest: _____

2. Having bright colors: _____

3. The act of moving: _____

4. A state of having no strength: _____

5. Full of peace: _____

6. Not having any use: _____

7. A state of tidiness: _____

8. The hard surface of a road or street: _____

▶ **Read each sentence. Write the correct word to complete it.**

1. If the kitchen looks neat and clean, it is _____ .
    wasteful   spotless

2. When a person tells exactly what happened in an event, the person is

being _____ .
    cheerful   truthful

Name _____

Suffix –ion

> **Use what you know about the suffix –ion to answer the questions below.**

1. If you gave someone directions, what did you do?

_____

_____

2. When might you need to take action at school?

_____

_____

3. If you were told to make a selection of something, what would you do?

_____

_____

4. Why might someone feel bad if they received a rejection?

_____

_____

5. What kinds of decorations would you see on your favorite holiday?

_____

_____

Name _____

Characters

Characters are the people and animals in a story. A character's development can contribute to the plot. When reading, pay attention to how a character acts, interacts with others, and changes to better understand the story.

> **Read page 88 of *Thunder Rose* and answer the questions.**

1. How does Tater change as a result of his interaction with Rose? How does this change contribute to the plot?

   _____

   _____

   _____

2. What does Rose do about the drought? What words and phrases show readers that Rose was determined to make it rain?

   _____

   _____

   _____

> **Read paragraphs 27–30 of *Thunder Rose* and answer the questions below.**

3. How does Rose react to the approaching tornadoes?

   _____

4. How does her reaction to the tornadoes compare to her reaction to the steer stampede earlier?

   _____

   _____

   _____

Name _____

Adages and Proverbs

Adages and proverbs are types of common expressions and sayings that have meanings beyond what can be understood by their individual words.

Adages are short statements that express a general truth or advice.

Proverbs are short sayings that have usually been around for centuries. They state a truth based on common sense or experiences.

▶ **Use paragraph 35 of *Thunder Rose* to answer the questions below.**

1. What does the adage "as thunder follows lightning, and sun follows rain" mean in this tall tale? How does this adage add to the meaning of the tale?

_____

_____

_____

_____

_____

2. Why might the author have chosen this adage to end *Thunder Rose*?

_____

_____

_____

3. Which of these sayings are adages or proverbs? Circle the adages and proverbs.

Look before you leap.

The clock strikes midnight.

Always get plenty of sleep.

The early bird gets the worm.

Absence makes the heart grow fonder.

Fill in the Blank: VCCV Pattern

> **Read the sentence. Choose a word from the box on the right that correctly completes the sentence. Write the word in the blank.**

million
collect
lumber
pepper
plastic
borrow
support
thirty
perfect
attend
canyon
traffic
fortune
danger
soccer
engine
picture
survive
seldom
effort

1. Charlie had collected so many stamps, it seemed like he had a

   _____ of them.

2. Juanita asked if she could _____ my book because she liked the pretty cover.

3. We are going to be late because all of the cars on the road have

   caused a lot of _____ .

4. Tina was excited because her family was going to visit the

   Grand _____ .

5. After dinner, Alex wanted to open his _____ cookie to find out what was written inside.

6. Despite being trapped on the mountain without food or water,

   the hikers were able to _____ for over a week.

7. Kayla's aunt put the pretty _____ she drew up on the refrigerator.

8. Airplanes have a very big _____ , which helps them stay in the sky.

Name _____

Critical Vocabulary

You can use the words you learn from reading as you talk and write.

> **Use your understanding of the Critical Vocabulary words from *In the Days of King Adobe* to support your answers to the questions below.**

1. Why might you be surprised if your **thrifty** neighbor went shopping every day? Explain.

   _____

   _____

2. What would you do if your aunt gave you a **generous** gift for your birthday?

   _____

   _____

3. Why might you receive an award for being a person of good **character**? Explain.

   _____

   _____

4. Would you be surprised if your kitten was **fascinated** by a ball of yarn? Why or why not?

   _____

   _____

> **Choose two of the Critical Vocabulary words and use them in a sentence.**

   _____

   _____

Name _____

Theme

Trickster tales and folktales often share a **theme**, an important message or lesson about life. Sometimes, this message or lesson is stated at the beginning or end of a story. More often, readers need to look for clues to determine a theme. When you read, look for details that show how the author develops the theme.

> **Answer the questions below after reading** *In the Days of King Adobe.*

1. What details does the author include to develop the theme of this folktale?

_____

_____

_____

_____

2. What is the author's theme or lesson to be learned from this trickster folktale?

_____

_____

3. Is the theme of this folktale stated or implied? Explain.

_____

_____

_____

Words with the VCCV Pattern

> **Basic 1–10. Write the word that completes each sentence.**

Word Bank
million
collect
lumber
pepper
plastic
borrow
support
thirty
perfect
attend
canyon
traffic
fortune
danger
soccer
engine
picture
survive
seldom
effort

1. We don't like swimming, so we _____ go to the pool.

2. Uncle Sam is busy, so he will not be able to _____ your concert.

3. Flora forgot her pencil, so she had to _____ one of mine.

4. Chicago is a big city, with almost three _____ people living in it.

5. Pablo's grandpa is a philatelist, which means he loves to _____ stamps.

6. The photographer took a beautiful _____ of the queen.

7. Jenny's mother put a lot of _____ into the special dinner.

8. In many other countries, the game of _____ is called football.

9. Beth loves to eat green _____ , but she doesn't like the red ones.

10. Jack's dad was late to work yesterday because he got stuck in _____ .

Name _____

Critical Vocabulary

You can use the words you learn from reading as you talk and write.

▷ **Use your understanding of the Critical Vocabulary words from *A Pair of Tricksters* to support your answers to the questions below. Then talk with a partner about your answers, using the Critical Vocabulary words.**

1. Cacti live in dry places, but they are very **succulent** on the inside. What else is succulent on the inside?

_____

_____

2. If you **clamped** something, what did you do?

_____

_____

▷ **Write a sentence using each of the Critical Vocabulary words below.**

_____

_____

Name _____

Figurative Language

Authors use language that helps readers picture a scene or feel a certain way. They may also use the sounds, such as alliteration and assonance, to connect ideas or to create phrases readers will remember. Figurative language helps readers better understand the meaning in a text.

Kind of Language	What It Is	Example
alliteration	repeating the beginning sound in words	*We could hear the rat-a-tat-tat of rain on the roof.*
assonance	repeating the vowel sound in words	*It's a treat to feel the heat.*

▶ **Reread page 118 of *Raven and Crayfish*. Then answer the questions.**

1. How does the author use alliteration in the text? Why?

_____

_____

_____

_____

2. How does the author use assonance, or repeated vowel sounds, in that phrase?

_____

_____

3. Why does the author repeat the alliteration at the end of the story?

_____

_____

4. Write a sentence using assonance or alliteration.

_____

Prefixes mis-, pre-, and dis-

> Use what you know about the prefixes to answer the questions below. Then use the underlined words as you talk with a partner about your answers.

1. What might happen if you <u>misbehave</u> at school?

_____

_____

2. Why might you need to <u>presoak</u> your clothes?

_____

_____

3. What would happen to a runner who was <u>disqualified</u> from a race?

_____

_____

> Write a sentence using each of the underlined words.

_____

_____

_____

Name _____

Characters

Characters are the people and animals in a story. Characters, along with other literary elements such as **events, conflicts,** and the **setting** all contribute to the **plot.**

▶ **Read page 115 of *The Fox and the Crow* to answer the questions below.**

1. What type of character is the Fox? Give examples from the text to support your answer.

_____

_____

_____

2. How might this experience change the Crow 's attitude about flatterers? Why do you think so?

_____

_____

_____

▶ **Read page 116 of *Raven and Crayfish* to answer the questions below.**

3. Who is the trickster? Explain.

_____

_____

_____

4. How is Raven different from Crow?

_____

_____

_____

Word Sort: VCV Pattern

▷ Are the words sorted correctly? Draw a line through the words that are in the wrong column. Write them in the correct column.

Short Vowel Sound	Long Vowel Sound
habit	polite
relay	events
planet	unite
rapid	punish
relief	detail
motel	frozen

▷ Use the words from the chart to fill in the blanks. Write the correct word on the line. Do the words have a short vowel sound or a long vowel sound? Circle the ones that have a short vowel sound.

1. Something you do over and over again becomes a _____ .

2. The goal of the meeting was to _____ people with different points of view.

3. The word _____ can mean a type of race or to pass messages along.

4. When something is _____ it happens very quickly.

Name _____

Critical Vocabulary

You can use the words you learn from reading as you talk and write.

▶ **Use your understanding of the Critical Vocabulary words from** *Ten Suns* **to support your answers to the questions below. Then use the Critical Vocabulary words as you talk with a partner about your answers.**

1. When have you shown **gratitude** to someone?

_____

2. If you saw flowers that had **withered**, would you give them to a friend? Why or why not?

_____

3. What would you feel if you touched something that was **scorching**?

_____

4. What would you consider **reckless** behavior?

_____

5. Think of a time you **assumed** something. What could you have done instead?

_____

_____

6. How do you think it would feel to **prosper**?

_____

▶ **Write a sentence using two of the Critical Vocabulary words.**

_____

_____

Name _____

Text and Graphic Features

> **Use the text and video versions of *Ten Suns* to answer the questions below.**

1. How does the illustration fit the description of Hu Yi?

_____

_____

_____

_____

2. How is this character portrayed in the video *The Ten Suns*?

_____

_____

> **Review the end of *Ten Suns* and think about the video.**

3. How does the video compare to the print version of this legend? What is the same? What is different?

_____

_____

_____

_____

4. What connections can you make between the text and the video *The Ten Suns*?

_____

_____

_____

Name _____

Suffixes –ity and –ty

> Complete the chart with words that contain the suffix –ity or –ty.

–ity	–ty

> Write a sentence for each word in the chart.

_____

_____

_____

_____

_____

_____

_____

_____

_____

Name _____

Media Techniques

The methods used to tell a story in video form are called **media techniques**.
Producers choose and combine different techniques to create the effects that best
tell the story.

Technique	What It Is
sound	voices, music, and other sound effects
voiceover	the voice of an unseen narrator who tells the story
visuals	all the types of images that viewers see
animation	a series of drawings or models that appear to move

When you watch a video, think about the choices the producer has made and how
these choices help viewers experience and understand important ideas.

> **Use the video and print versions of the Ten Suns legend to answer the
> questions below.**

1. How are the illustrations in the video different from those in the text?

_____

_____

2. How do the sound effects and visuals in the video add to this tale?

_____

_____

3. How does the animation in the video help you understand this legend?

_____

_____

_____

Name _____

Words with VCV Syllable Division Pattern

> Read each sentence. Underline the word with the VCV pattern.

1. The tornado siren is tested once a month.

2. We left our classroom the moment school was over.

3. We live on the planet Earth.

4. Our music festival occurs in April.

5. On field day we have many relay races.

6. It was a big relief when the test was over.

7. I have a habit of talking to myself.

8. Raoul has a great sense of humor.

9. Every detail of the book fair was organized.

10. We stayed at a nice motel on our trip.

Literary Elements

Stories are developed through **literary elements** such as **plot, characters,** and **setting.** The characters, setting, and events contribute to the development of the story's plot.

▶ **Read *Ten Suns*, pages 125–128. Then answer the questions below.**

1. Why do the boys decide to change their routine of walking across the sky?

_____

_____

2. Why do the boys get up early?

_____

_____

3. What problems do the boys' actions cause?

_____

_____

4. Do you think the boys realize their power will be damaging?

_____

_____

▶ **Think about the events in this legend.**

5. With a partner, retell the events of the plot in chronological order.

_____

_____

_____

_____

Name _____

VCCV and VCV Syllable Division Patterns

> Read each sentence. If the underlined word has a VCCV syllable pattern, write the word in the first column. If it has a VCV syllable pattern, write it in the second column.

VCCV	VCV

1. We will go shopping <u>after</u> we eat breakfast.

2. Our new <u>baby</u> is three weeks old.

3. Only one blueberry <u>muffin</u> was left on the tray.

4. The puppies are playing in the <u>basket</u>.

5. Our family had a <u>picnic</u> in the park.

6. Ten is an <u>even</u> number.

7. The <u>lady</u> wore a pretty red dress.

8. The beautiful <u>hotel</u> was very old.

Critical Vocabulary

You can use the words you learn from reading as you talk and write.

▶ **Use your understanding of the Critical Vocabulary words to help you finish each sentence.**

1. A flashlight is **convenient** to have when _____ .

2. Tonight's homework is time-**intensive** because _____ .

3. It was hard to stay **hydrated** yesterday because _____ .

4. We **transported** baked goods to the picnic in _____

_____ .

5. We used **disposable** plates and cups because _____

_____ .

6. One way to **assess** what you need for a trip is _____

_____ .

7. The article had a big **impact** because _____

_____ .

▶ **Choose two of the Critical Vocabulary words and use them in a sentence.**

_____

_____

Author's Purpose

An **author's purpose** is his or her reason for writing. The author may have a **perspective,** or attitude, about his or her topic. When you read, look for the evidence an author provides to support his or her perspective.

▶ **Reread the second box on page 154 in** *Eco-Friendly Food.* **Then answer the questions.**

1. Who do you think the author's intended audience is?

_____

_____

2. What is the author's perspective, or attitude, about disposable containers? Use evidence for support.

_____

_____

_____

▶ **Reread page 160. Then answer the questions below.**

3. What is the purpose of the text on page 160?

_____

_____

4. What is the author's perspective about the topic of this text?

_____

_____

Name _____

VCCV and VCV Syllable Division Patterns

▶ Circle all words in the row having the same first vowel sound as the boldfaced word.

1. **basket**	magnet	appoint	napkin	master
2. **publish**	rubber	supper	bundle	super
3. **fifteen**	lilac	minor	kitten	pillow
4. **yellow**	message	began	female	rescue
5. **okay**	local	open	solid	solo
6. **bacon**	attic	navy	banner	table
7. **eagle**	before	gentle	even	errand
8. **silent**	window	item	title	tiger
9. **costume**	bottom	locate	clover	cotton
10. **music**	unicorn	number	public	unite

Name _____

Latin Roots *port*, *dict*

The word *transported* contains the root *port* meaning "to carry."

The word *predict* contains the root *dict* meaning "to speak."

> Complete the chart with other words that contain the roots *port* and *dict*.

port	*dict*

> Write a sentence for 4 words in the chart.

_____

_____

_____

_____

_____

_____

_____

Name _____

Ideas and Support

When authors present **ideas** and claims, they **support** them with facts, reasons, and other evidence. Evaluate the way an author supports an idea or claim by determining which statements are facts and which are opinions.

▷ **Reread paragraphs 5–6 of *Eco-Friendly Food*. Then answer the questions below.**

1. What is the author's claim about these foods?

_____

2. What evidence does the author use to support this claim?

_____

_____

3. What evidence does the author use to argue against this claim?

_____

▷ **Reread paragraph 10. Then answer the questions below.**

4. What is the author's claim?

_____

_____

5. What are the reasons the author gives to support this claim?

_____

_____

6. Who is the intended audience?

_____

Name _____

Text and Graphic Features

Authors of informational text often use **text and graphic features** to help organize the information, highlight key ideas, and support readers' understanding of the text. They use boldfaced words, headings, photographs, diagrams, charts, and graphs to help readers better understand the important ideas in a text.

> ▶ **Answer the questions about paragraph 7 and the sidebar on page 157 of** *Eco-Friendly Food.*

1. What is the author's claim about bottled drinks?

_____

_____

2. How does the information in the sidebar support the author's claim?

_____

_____

_____

> ▶ **Reread page 159. Then answer the questions below.**

3. Why is the text on page 159 numbered?

_____

_____

4. What do the diagrams show?

_____

5. Why do you think the author includes these visuals?

_____

6. How do these diagrams support your understanding of a cylinder garden?

_____

Name _____

Words with the VCCV Syllable Division Pattern

▶ Complete each sentence with the best word from the word box. Then divide the word into syllables.

declare	whether	secret	apron	poster
degree	achieve	whiskers	chicken	bushel
ticket	author	rocket	gather	rather

1. Carla asked _____ the muffins were ready to eat.

2. The cat's _____ tickle my arm.

3. I suggest you wear this _____ before you start cooking.

4. Homemade _____ soup was cooking on the stove.

5. Gov. Smith will _____ the flooded land a disaster area.

6. We picked a _____ of apples from that tree.

7. A good writer will _____ information about a subject before writing.

8. The _____ has been on our classroom wall all year.

9. When my brother graduates from college he will earn a _____ .

10. O. Henry was a famous _____ of short stories.

Name _____

Critical Vocabulary

You can use the words you learn from reading as you talk and write.

> Use your understanding of the Critical Vocabulary words to complete a word web for each word. Write words and phrases in the outer ovals that are related to the word in the center. Discuss your word webs with a partner.

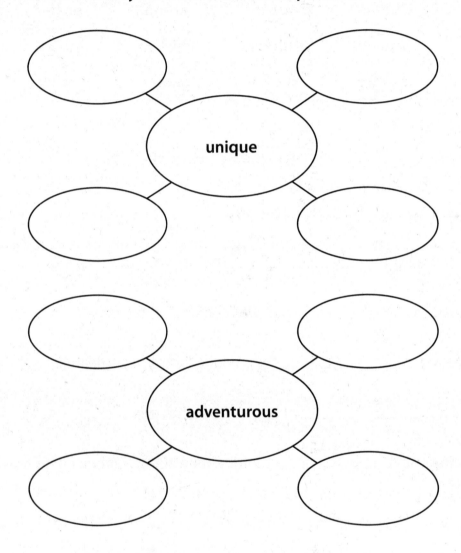

> Use each of the Critical Vocabulary words in a sentence.

_____

_____

Name _____

Media Techniques

Media techniques include visual elements, such as action scenes, close-up views, and text boxes. Sound elements include narration. The narration is an important element in an informational video. The narrator needs to be an expert or someone who knows the topic well so that the viewer receives the correct information.

▶ **Review the visual elements in** *Kids Rock Nutrition in the Kitchen*. **Then answer the questions below.**

1. Is the adult cook an expert in food preparation? How do you know?

_____

_____

_____

2. Why do you think the video includes close-up views of a variety of vegetables?

_____

_____

_____

3. If chicken takes longer to bake than fish, why can both types of packets be in the oven together and be fully cooked at the same time? Cite information from the video to support your answer.

_____

_____

_____

Name _____

Words with the VCCV Syllable Division Pattern

▷ Draw a line between the syllables in the following VCCV words. Then write the words in the correct column.

puffin	declare	pocket	degree	rather
secret	clothing	tether	agree	monkey
gathering	rescuing	winter	poster	publishing
achievable	confide	subject	whether	apron

V / CCV	VCC / V	VC / CV

Name _____

Critical Vocabulary

You can use the words you learn from reading as you talk and write.

> **Use your understanding of the Critical Vocabulary words to tell which sentence best fits the meaning of the bold word.**

1. pests   Those little mice are so adorable!

Mice got into the house and ate our cereal.

2. edible   These mushrooms are delicious.

These mushrooms are poisonous.

3. forbidden   I always have an apple for my after-school snack.

I am not allowed to eat sweets before dinner.

4. attitudes   Some people have strong ideas about the food they eat.

Some people enjoy watching cooking shows.

> **Choose two of the Critical Vocabulary words and use them in a sentence.**

_____

_____

_____

_____

Name _____

Central Idea

The **central idea** of a text is the most important idea the author wants readers to understand. Relevant details are the facts, examples, and other evidence that support the central idea.

> **Reread the section headed "Bugs Do a Body Good" on page 174 of** *Bug Bites* **to answer questions 1–3.**

1. What is the central idea of this section?

_____

_____

_____

2. What are two relevant, or important, details that support the central idea?

_____

_____

_____

3. How does the author organize the details in this section? How does the organization support the central idea?

_____

_____

_____

Name _____

Prefixes sub-, fore-

▶ Complete the chart with words that contain the prefixes *sub–* and *fore–*.

sub–	*fore–*

▶ Write a sentence for four words in the chart.

_____

_____

_____

_____

_____

_____

_____

Name _____

Ideas and Support

In an argumentative text, an author states a **claim**. The author provides facts or examples to support his or her claim. Sometimes an author will express a **perspective**. The perspective tells what the author thinks or feels about a subject and is supported by examples in the text.

▸ **Reread paragraphs 5 and 6 on page 173 in *Bug Bites* to answer the questions.**

1. What claim does the author make?

_____

2. What evidence does the author provide to support this claim?

_____

_____

_____

▸ **Reread page 176 to answer the questions.**

3. How does the author support his perspective on eating bugs?

_____

_____

_____

4. What readers do you think the author had in mind when writing this text? What evidence supports this idea?

_____

_____

_____

Name _____

Words with the VCCCV Syllable Division Pattern

> Circle the consonant blend or digraph in each VCCCV word. Then divide the words into syllables and write the words in the correct column.

mischief	hundred	purchase	harmless
kingdom	athlete	although	explain
complete	middle	monster	supply

VC / CCV	VCC / CV

Name _____

Critical Vocabulary

You can use the words you learn from reading as you talk and write.

▶ **Use your understanding of the Critical Vocabulary words to support your answers to the questions below. Then talk with a partner about your answers, using the Critical Vocabulary words.**

1. What kind of **culinary** skills do you have?

_____

2. What would you be **astounded** to see at school?

_____

3. Why might you be **crestfallen** after a game?

_____

4. What recipe would you **opt** to make for a cook-off?

_____

5. Why might a friend take **offense** at what you did?

_____

6. What do you think is **luscious**?

_____

7. How would you **react** if a pet snake got out of its cage?

_____

▶ **Write a sentence below using two Critical Vocabulary words.**

_____

_____

Name _____

Text and Graphic Features

Text features can present important parts of a story. Different kinds of type and punctuation may be used by an author to communicate something important or to get the reader's attention.

Graphic features are visuals, such as illustrations, diagrams, maps, and speech bubbles that help explain ideas in a text. In stories, graphic features may provide more details that were not provided to the reader in the story itself.

> **Answer the questions about page 188 of** *Now You're Cooking!*

1. What facial expression does each character have?

_____

2. How do the illustrations add to your understanding of the story?

_____

_____

_____

> **Answer the question about page 190 of** *Now You're Cooking!*

3. How do the text features on this page help readers understand the recipe?

_____

_____

_____

Name _____

Greek Roots meter, therm, phon, tele, scope

> Complete the chart with words that use the Greek roots *meter, therm, phon, tele,* and *scope*. Sample responses are shown.

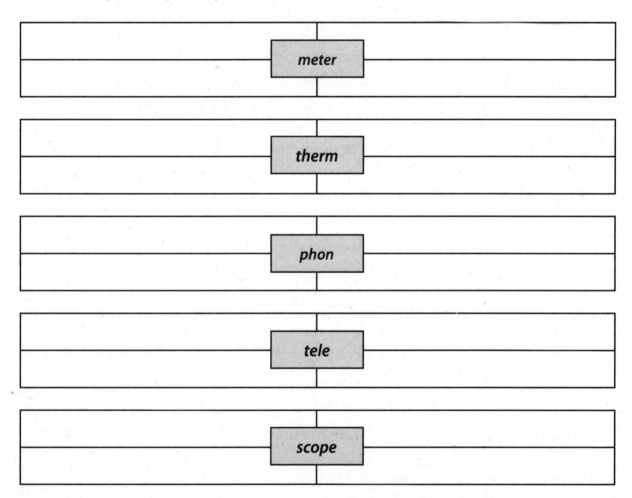

> Write a sentence using one of the words from each category.

_____

_____

_____

_____

_____

Idioms

An **idiom** is a phrase that means something different from what the individual words say. Idioms can make a story or text more interesting to read.

Examples: *a dime a dozen; a bee in your bonnet*

▶ **Reread paragraph 2 of *Now You're Cooking!* Then answer the question.**

1. What does Avani mean when she uses the idiom "Now you're cooking"?

_____

_____

▶ **Answer the questions about paragraph 4 on page 184 of the story.**

2. What does the idiom "my goose is cooked" mean?

_____

3. What clues in the text help you understand the idiom?

_____

_____

▶ **Answer the questions about paragraphs 16–17.**

4. What does the idiom "cook circles around you" mean?

_____

5. What does this idiom demonstrate in regard to how Martina is feeling about competing?

_____

Name _____

Words with VCCCV Syllable Division Pattern

> Underline the consonant blend or consonant digraph in the VCCCV pattern. Then write the word dividing it into syllables.

1. pilgrim _____ _____

2. sandwich _____ _____

3. orchard _____ _____

4. surprise _____ _____

5. turtle _____ _____

6. single _____ _____

7. farther _____ _____

8. sample _____ _____

> Choose four of the words and use them in sentences.

_____

_____

_____

_____

Name _____

Point of View

When you read a story, you need to know who the narrator, or storyteller, is. It's important to know from whose **point of view** the events are told because different people can tell the same story different ways.

First-Person Point of View The narrator . . .	Third-Person Point of View The narrator . . .
is a character in the story.	is someone outside the story.
tells his or her own thoughts and feelings.	tells the thoughts and feelings of others.
uses pronouns such as *I*, *me*, *my*, *mine*, and *we*.	uses pronouns such as *he*, *she*, *him*, *her*, *his*, *hers*, *they*, *them*, and *their*.

> **Answer the questions about page 183 of** *Now You're Cooking!*

1. From which point of view is paragraph 1 being told?

_____

_____

2. Why do you think the author writes the story in the third person?

_____

_____

> **Answer the question about page 189 of** *Now You're Cooking!*

3. How does the point of view affect what you learn about the characters?

_____

_____

Name _____

Words with VV Syllable Division Pattern

> Read each sentence. Underline the word with the VV syllable division pattern in each sentence.

1. I'm afraid the rain will ruin your new hat.

2. The babies will sleep more easily in a quiet room.

3. "There will be a meteor shower next week," the news anchor stated.

4. The bear roamed the camping area looking for food.

5. The teachers will announce the winner of the poetry contest tomorrow.

> Underline the correct way to divide each boldfaced word into syllables.

1. dial	dia l	di al	d ial
2. violet	vi o let	vi olet	vio let
3. meow	me ow	me o w	meo w
4. science	sci en ce	scien ce	sci ence
5. diary	dia ry	di a ry	di ary

Name _____

Critical Vocabulary

You can use the words you learn from reading as you talk and write.

> **Use your understanding of the Critical Vocabulary words to support your answers to the questions below.**

1. One meaning of the word **oasis** is a pool of water in the desert. How is this meaning like a park in a dirty city?

   _____

   _____

2. For what kind of project would you need **permission** from the school principal?

   _____

   _____

3. Why might someone be **installing** things in an **abandoned** house?

   _____

   _____

4. If you could choose a **frequent** activity, what would you choose and why?

   _____

   _____

5. How much daily exercise do you think is **sufficient** for someone your age?

   _____

> **Choose two of the Critical Vocabulary words and use them in a sentence. Include a synonym or antonym for one of the words.**

   _____

   _____

Name _____

Text and Graphic Features

In a graphic novel, text is used either as narration or as speech. Visuals such as diagrams and illustrations help explain ideas in the text.

> ▶ **Answer the questions about page 218 in *Luz Sees the Light*.**

1. Which text on the page is narration?

_____

_____

2. What purpose does this narration serve in the story?

_____

_____

3. What purpose do the drawings and speech balloons serve in this part of the story?

_____

_____

> ▶ **Answer the question about page 227 in *Luz Sees the Light*.**

4. What are three different ways in which text is used on this page?

_____

_____

Name _____

Words with VV Syllable Division Pattern

▶ **Read each sentence. Complete the sentence by choosing the word with the VV syllable division pattern. With this pattern both vowels are sounded.**

1. Students can learn to skate by looking at this _____ .
pamphlet   video

2. The child's toy was made of _____ plastic.
pliable   flexible

3. Thelma is studying to be a _____ .
dentist   librarian

4. The _____ was closed for remodeling.
theater   hotel

5. Tyrone loves to read books on _____ .
biology   chemistry

▶ **Read the words in the box aloud. Circle all of the words in which you hear two different vowel sounds in the VV pattern.**

refrain	teach	screen	dear	triumph
reality	break	diagram	could	trial
fluid	gradual	serial	explain	pail
pioneer	create	food	diet	client

Name _____

Using Suffixes –ible and –able

The suffixes –*ible* and –*able* mean "able to" or "likely to" do or be something. They are used frequently in English words, usually after verbs, such as *believable* and *collapsible*.

> **Complete the chart with other words that contain the suffix –*ible* or –*able*.**

–ible	–able

> **Write a sentence for each word in the chart.**

_____

_____

_____

_____

_____

_____

_____

_____

_____

_____

Name _____

Theme

Knowing the **theme** helps you understand the main message of a story. How characters respond to situations can help readers see how the theme is developed.

▶ **Answer the questions about page 210 in *Luz Sees the Light*.**

1. How does Luz want to change the empty lot?

_____

_____

2. What can you infer about the theme of the story from Luz's statement?

_____

_____

▶ **Answer the questions about page 232.**

3. How do Luz's words help you determine the theme?

_____

_____

4. How does knowing the theme help you better understand the story events?

_____

_____

Name _____

Idioms

An **idiom** is an expression that means something different from the meaning of its individual words. Knowing how to identify idioms helps you understand the meaning of a text.

▶ **Answer the questions about the idiom on page 217 in *Luz Sees the Light*.**

1. What does the idiom "out to lunch" mean?

_____

_____

2. What clues in the text help you understand the idiom?

_____

_____

▶ **Reread the middle row on page 222. Then answer the questions.**

3. What does the idiom "on board" mean?

_____

_____

4. What clues in the text help you understand the idiom?

_____

_____

Final Schwa + /r/ Sound

beggar	finger	birdwatcher	cedar	traitor	sugar
doctor	partner	visitor	enter	actor	fever
teacher	author	polar	harbor	cellar	banner

Across

3. any one of five digits on a hand

6. to go into a place

9. medical person who treats patients

10. an underground room

11. place where ships dock

12. a flag

Down

1. a high rise in body temperature

2. food item used to sweeten something

4. an evergreen tree

5. person who observes birds

7. person who betrays his country

8. having to do with the North or South Pole

Name _____

Critical Vocabulary

You can use the words you learn from reading as you talk and write.

▶ **Use your understanding of the Critical Vocabulary words to support your answers to the questions below.**

1. What are you **obsessed** with? Why?

_____

2. Why do teachers give little children **blunt** scissors to use?

_____

_____

3. If you passed a door marked "Army **Recruiting**," what would you think they probably do there?

_____

_____

4. Would you like to be **appointed** to help plan a class party? Why or why not?

_____

_____

5. What might cause a sea creature to become **stranded** and **disoriented** on the shore?

_____

_____

▶ **Choose two of the Critical Vocabulary words and use them in a sentence. Include either a synonym or an antonym of the vocabulary word in the sentence.**

_____

_____

194

Figurative Language

When authors use **figurative language**, they use words and phrases that have meanings beyond their literal meanings.

	What It Is	**Example**
Sensory Language	words that tell how something looks, sounds, feels, tastes, or smells	*scorching hot sand*
Simile	comparing two things using *like* or *as*	*a shell* as *smooth* as *glass*
Metaphor	comparing two things without using *like* or *as*	*a maze of city streets*
Alliteration	repeating the same sounds or letters at the beginning of words	*two tiny turtles*

> Answer the questions about page 245 in *On Sea Turtle Patrol*.

1. What simile describes how Callie feels as she runs?

_____

2. What does the simile mean?

_____

3. Which sensory details describe what the first boy on the bike looks like?

_____

4. How does this description contribute to the meaning of the text?

_____

_____

> Answer the question about paragraph 52 on page 247 in *On Sea Turtle Patrol*.

5. How does the alliteration "floating free" contribute to the meaning of the story?

_____

Name _____

Final Syllable (r-controlled vowel)
Final Schwa + /r/ Sound

> Add **er, ar,** or **or** to each base word.

contract	pill	command
beg	publish	direct
develop	sail	cell

> Then sort the words by the spelling of the final schwa + /r/ sound.

–*ar*	–*er*	–*or*

Name _____

Critical Vocabulary

You can use the words you learn from reading as you talk and write.

▷ **Use your understanding of the Critical Vocabulary words to support your answers to the questions below. Then use the Critical Vocabulary words as you talk with a partner about your answers.**

1. When and why is it important to **estimate**?

_____

_____

_____

2. If someone said, "I wish things wouldn't **decay**," what would you tell them?

_____

_____

_____

▷ **Use the two Critical Vocabulary words in a sentence. Include either a synonym or an antonym of the vocabulary word in the sentence.**

_____

_____

_____

_____

_____

_____

Name _____

Text and Graphic Features

In nonfiction texts, authors may include **text and graphic features** such as headings, captions, and graphs to help readers understand the meaning of the text.

Feature	What It Is
Headings	type that is larger than other text; may be a different color
Captions	text that appears near a photograph or other image
Graphs	images that show connections between amounts

▶ **Answer the questions about pages 254–255 of** *How Can We Reduce Household Waste?*

1. How does the author use headings to organize the story?

_____

_____

2. How does the circle graph on page 254 connect to the text?

_____

3. How do the caption and photograph at the top of page 255 work together to contribute to the ideas in the text?

_____

_____

▶ **Answer the question about the graph on page 268.**

4. How does the graph add to your understanding of the text on page 268?

_____

_____

Name _____

Using Suffixes –*ful*, –*ous*, –*less*

The suffix –*ful* means "full of." The suffix –*ous* means "having" or "possessing." The suffix –*less* means "without."

> Complete the chart with words that contain the suffix –*ful*, –*ous*, or –*less*.

–ful	–ous	–less

> Write a sentence for six of the words in the chart.

_____

_____

_____

_____

_____

_____

_____

_____

_____

_____

_____

Name _____

Ideas and Support

When authors write an argumentative text, they present a **claim**. Authors **support**, or back up, their claim with reasons and evidence.

Authors provide evidence to show that their reasons make sense. A **fact** is a statement that is true and can be proved. Facts help readers understand why they should agree with a claim.

> **Answer the questions about paragraphs 24 and 25 of** *How Can We Reduce Household Waste?*

1. What claim does the author make?

_____

2. What reasons or evidence does the author provide to support this claim?

_____

_____

> **Reread paragraph 29 of** *How Can We Reduce Household Waste?*

3. What claim does the author make about reusing items? What reasons does the author give to support this claim?

_____

_____

Words with Final Stable Syllable
Final Schwa + /l/ Sound

1. Complete this story by writing in each blank the correct word with the indicated final schwa + /l/ sound from the word box.

eagle	article	barrel	animal	gentle
metal	squirrel	special	marvel	coastal

My teacher asked me to write an _____ [-*le*] for our class newspaper.

I wasn't sure what to write about. Maybe I could write a story about an _____

[-*al*]. There are many different ones to choose from. I thought about our rabbit, which

is _____ [-*le*]. Then I thought about a _____ [-*el*] with its nest of acorns.

Should I research our nation's symbol, the _____ [-*le*]? Or would a _____ [-*al*]

bird like the pelican make my writing _____ [-*al*]?

2. Write two or more sentences telling which animal you think the author should choose. Include three words with the final schwa + /l/ sound. Underline the letters that make the final schwa sound in each word.

_____

_____

_____

_____

Name _____

Critical Vocabulary

You can use the words you learn from reading as you talk and write.

> **Use your understanding of the Critical Vocabulary words to support your answers to the questions below.**

1. If someone asked, "Who were your **ancestors**?" what would you say?

_____

_____

2. If you drew a picture of a **swirl**, what would it look like?

_____

_____

3. Would you swim in water that had fast **currents**? Why or why not?

_____

_____

4. Why might someone **sneer** at an **outspoken** person?

_____

_____

5. How do you **envision** a **canopy** of trees? How does it move?

_____

_____

> **Choose two of the Critical Vocabulary words and use them in a sentence.**

_____

_____

Name _____

Author's Craft

Author's craft can include figurative language and anecdotes to contribute to the meaning of the text.

> **Reread page 274 in *Seeds of Change*, and then answer the questions below.**

1. Why does the author begin the biography with this anecdote?

_____

_____

2. What figurative language does the author use? How does this add meaning to the text?

_____

_____

_____

_____

> **Reread paragraph 10 in *Seeds of Change*. Answer the question.**

3. How does the author's use of similes help you understand Wangari's focus on her brother's teaching?

_____

_____

> **Reread paragraph 41. Then answer the question.**

4. Why does the author include this section? How is this section different?

_____

_____

Name _____

Using Suffixes –ic, –en

The suffix –ic means "of or relating to." The suffix –en means "to give or have the characteristics."

▶ **Complete the chart with words that contain the suffix –ic or –en.**

–ic	–en

▶ **Write a sentence for each word in the chart.**

_____

_____

_____

_____

_____

_____

_____

_____

_____

_____

_____

Name _____

Literary Elements

Biographies contain **literary elements,** such as people, settings, and events. Identifying and analyzing these elements can help you better understand a biography.

▶ **Revisit pages 278–279 in** *Seeds of Change.* **Then answer the questions.**

1. Who is this biography about?

_____

2. Who are some secondary characters? Why have these people been the focus of the biography so far?

_____

_____

_____

▶ **Answer the questions about pages 282 and 283 in** *Seeds of Change.*

3. What is the setting in this illustration?

_____

_____

4. What details from the text support your thinking?

_____

_____

_____

Name _____

Words with Final Schwa + /l/ Sound

> **Choose the word with the schwa + /l/ sound to complete the sentence. Write it in the blank and underline the letters that stand for the final schwa + /l/ sound.**

1. The _____ was filled with rainwater.
       bucket   barrel

2. The _____ clown juggled six balls at once.
       carnival   circus

3. The prince lived in a _____ surrounded by a moat.
       castle   mansion

4. The _____ vase broke when it hit the floor.
       glass   crystal

5. The snowflakes _____ as they float down from the sky.
       sparkle   glisten

6. My _____ is very obedient and always sits when I tell her to.
       poodle   puppy

7. Jane has a tea _____ that whistles when water boils.
       pitcher   kettle

8. A kitten is a _____ pet for children.
       gentle   lovely

Name _____

Text Structure

Authors organize texts in many different ways. Paying attention to **text structure** can help a reader better understand the text.

▶ **Reread pages 278 and 281 in** *Seeds of Change*. **Then answer the question.**

1. How has the author organized the information on these pages? Explain.

_____

_____

_____

▶ **Answer the questions about page 282 of** *Seeds of Change*.

2. What important events occur in Wangari's life after she starts school in the city? What text structure does the author use to tell these events?

_____

_____

_____

_____

3. Why does the author include all these events?

_____

_____

_____

Name _____

Multisyllabic Words

▸ **Read each sentence. Choose the three-syllable word that correctly completes the sentence. Write the word on the line. Then divide the word into syllables.**

1. My sister loves that movie because it is the _____ .
scariest   nicest   cutest

2. Sasha likes to play the _____ in the school band.
trumpet   flute   clarinet

3. There is a famous _____ on the island.
mountain   plateau   volcano

4. Joe's favorite food is _____ and meatballs.
spaghetti   pepperoni   noodles

5. Junko's favorite school subject is _____ .
mathematics   history   geometry

6. Inez's father traveled to Spain for _____ .
vacation   business   health

7. It's raining, so Mom told me to take my _____ .
umbrella   poncho   raincoat

8. Smile, so the _____ can take your picture.
artist   camera   photographer

9. When is Carla going to the _____ ?
movies   celebration   festival

Name _____

Critical Vocabulary

You can use the words you learn from reading as you talk and write.

▶ **Use your understanding of the Critical Vocabulary words to support your answers to the questions below. Then use the Critical Vocabulary words as you talk with a partner about your answers.**

1. What single item would **significantly** improve your life?

_____

_____

2. What person has **enabled** you to do something you would not have done on your own?

_____

_____

3. If you could own the **patent** for something, what would it be?

_____

_____

4. What would be a **peak** experience for you?

_____

_____

5. What message would you want **transmitted** to your best friend?

_____

_____

Name _____

6. What flowers should *not* be **plucked**?

_____

_____

7. If you **proposed** a movie to watch tonight, what movie would it be?

_____

_____

8. If you wanted to run for class president, how would you **influence** others to vote for you?

_____

_____

▶ **Write sentences below using two Critical Vocabulary words.**

_____

_____

Name _____

Text Structure

Text structure refers to how the information in a text is organized. A chronological text structure tells events in the order in which they happened. When authors organize by description, a central idea is stated at the beginning of a section of text. The author then elaborates on the central idea with facts and examples.

> **Answer the questions about pages 310–311 in *The History of Communication*.**

1. What is the text structure of paragraphs 22–25? How do you know?

_____

_____

2. How does knowing the text structure help you understand the ideas in paragraphs 22–25?

_____

_____

> **Answer the questions about pages 312–313 in *The History of Communication*.**

3. What text structure does the author use in this section?

_____

4. How does this text structure help readers understand the ideas in this section?

_____

_____

_____

_____

_____

Multisyllabic Words

▷ **Choose the correct syllabication for each word. Underline the stressed syllable.**

1. po ta to   pot at o   po tat o

2. glo ri ous   glor i ous   glori ous

3. im port ant   imp or tant   im por tant

4. re new al   renew al   re ne wal

5. exam ple   ex amp le   ex am ple

6. vert i cal   ver ti cal   ver tic al

7. mus i cal   mu si cal   mu sic al

8. exc ell ent   excel lent   ex cel lent

Name _____

Latin Roots tele, port, graph

The roots *tele*, *port*, and *graph* have Latin origins.

The meaning of the root *tele* is "at a distance."

The meaning of the root *port* is "to carry."

The meaning of the root *graph* is "to write."

> Complete the chart with words that contain the roots *tele*, *port*, and *graph*.

tele	port	graph

> Write a sentence each for three of the words in the chart.

_____

_____

_____

_____

_____

_____

_____

_____

_____

Name _____

Central Idea

The **central idea** in a text is the most important idea the author wants the reader to think about. The author supports the central idea with relevant, or important, details.

> **Answer the questions about pages 306–307 in _The History of Communication_.**

1. What is the central idea of the section "The Telegraph"?

_____

_____

2. What relevant details in the text support the central idea?

_____

_____

_____

> **Answer the questions about pages 316–317 in _The History of Communication_.**

3. What is the central idea of the section "The Internet"?

_____

_____

4. What relevant details support this idea?

_____

_____

_____

_____

Name _____

Text and Graphic Features

Informational text often includes **text features** such as headings and captions. Informational text usually includes one or more **graphic features** such as photographs, diagrams, and illustrations.

▶ **Revisit page 309 in *The History of Communication*. Then answer the questions.**

1. What unique text or graphic feature do you notice on this page? What information does it give? How does this information contribute to the text?

_____

_____

▶ **Reread paragraph 25 in *The History of Communication*. Then answer the question.**

2. How do the photograph and caption at the top of page 311 connect to the text? How do the photograph and caption add to your understanding of the ideas in the text?

_____

_____

▶ **Reread pages 312–313 and answer the questions.**

3. How do the diagrams and captions on page 312 connect to the text in paragraph 30?

_____

4. How do the diagrams and captions add to your understanding of the text?

_____

_____

Name _____

Words with Silent Consonants

▶ Complete the crossword puzzle using words from the word box.
Circle the silent consonant in each word.

handsome	
comb	
wreath	
half	
limb	
kneel	
tomb	
gnarled	
wrestled	
fetch	
listen	
history	
yolk	
calm	
folktale	
plumber	
honest	
doubt	

Across

 4. pay attention to a speaker

 5. quiet and peaceful

 8. to be uncertain about something

 9. someone who always tells the truth

 11. a branch of the tree

Down

 1. flowers and greenery arranged in a circle

 2. the yellow part of an egg

 3. twisted and tangled; not straight

 5. make hair smooth and neat

 6. to go get something

 7. a story passed down through the years

 10. a burial place

Name _____

Critical Vocabulary

You can use the words you learn from reading as you talk and write.

> **Use your understanding of the Critical Vocabulary words to support your answers to the questions below. Then use the Critical Vocabulary words as you talk with a partner about your answers.**

1. What kind of new technology might cause widespread **astonishment**? Explain.

_____

_____

2. Do you think **gestures** are an important part of public speaking? Why or why not?

_____

_____

3. What do **linguists** study?

_____

_____

4. Humans have an **instinct** to communicate. What **instincts** do animals have?

_____

_____

> **Write a sentence below using two Critical Vocabulary words.**

_____

_____

Name _____

Words with Silent Consonants

▶ Choose the correct word from the word box to complete each sentence. Underline the silent consonant in the word.

climb	wreath	gnarled	listen	knuckle
handsome	hasten	wrinkle	comb	yolk
calm	tomb	answer	honest	fetch
folktale	limb	half	plumber	kneel

1. The girl wore a beautiful _____ of flowers in her hair.

2. Our teacher read us a _____ from Germany.

3. When the sink was stopped up, we called a _____ .

4. The _____ old tree in the town square was a hundred years old.

5. Our group must _____ if we want to make the meeting.

6. A _____ is a handy thing to carry in a pocket.

7. The twins taught their dog, Sparky, to _____ .

8. An _____ person is worthy of respect.

9. George could not figure out the _____ to my riddle.

10. A leopard is able to _____ a tree.

Name _____

Critical Vocabulary

You can use the words you learn from reading as you talk and write.

> **Use your understanding of the Critical Vocabulary words to support your answers to the questions below. Then use the Critical Vocabulary words as you talk with a partner about your answers.**

1. How would you design a backpack so that it was both **practical** and stylish?

_____

_____

2. When might a simple task seem like a major **operation**?

_____

_____

3. How important is it for your clothing to be **immaculate**?

_____

_____

> **Write a sentence below using two Critical Vocabulary words.**

_____

_____

_____

_____

Name _____

Central Idea

Authors organize their writing in ways that help readers understand their most important ideas.

- The **central idea** is the most important idea in a text. An author may state the central idea directly, or it may be suggested by the details.
- Relevant, or important, details tell more about the central idea. They can explain, describe, or provide examples that help to support the central idea. The kind of details an author includes depends on how the text is organized.

> **Answer the questions about the central idea and relevant details in the video _Dolphin Dinner_.**

1. What is the central idea of this video?

_____

_____

2. What are two relevant details that support this idea?

_____

_____

3. How is the video organized, and how does its structure support the central idea?

_____

_____

Name _____

Prefixes *il-*, *ir-*

The prefix *il-* or *ir-* placed at the beginning of a word changes the meaning of the word to its opposite.

▶ **Complete the chart with words that contain the prefixes *il-* or *ir-*.**

il-	*ir-*

▶ **Write a sentence each for three of the words in the chart.**

_____

_____

_____

_____

_____

_____

_____

_____

_____

_____

_____

_____

Name _____

Media Techniques

The methods used to tell a story in video form are called **media techniques**. Producers choose and combine different techniques to create the effects that best tell the story.

Technique	What It Is
sound	voices, music, and other sound effects
voice-over	the voice of an unseen narrator who tells the story
visuals	all the types of images that viewers see
live action	real people and animals who are part of the action
animation	a series of drawings or models that appear to move

When you watch a video, think about the choices the producer has made and how those choices help viewers experience and understand important ideas.

> **Answer the questions about the media techniques used in *Dolphin Dinner*.**

1. Which media techniques does this video use?

_____

2. How does the music support the events in the video? Explain.

_____

_____

_____

3. How do the media techniques support the video's purpose?

_____

_____

Name _____

Unusual Spelling Patterns

▶ Choose a word in each row that has the same vowel sound as the bold letters in the first word.

1. unpl**ea**sant   necktie   seaplane   eyelid

2. dis**gui**se   rebirth   realize   rebuild

3. unfortun**ate**   celebrate   flashlight   bandit

4. reb**uild**   unfilled   refined   retried

5. re**new**al   refused   disputed   unloosened

▶ Use the first word in each row in an original sentence.

_____

_____

_____

_____

_____

_____

_____

_____

_____

Name _____

Critical Vocabulary

You can use the words you learn from reading as you talk and write.

▶ **Use your understanding of the Critical Vocabulary words to support your answers to the questions below. Then use the Critical Vocabulary words as you talk with a partner about your answers.**

1. Why might you want to thoroughly **inspect** your surroundings before choosing a picnic spot?

   _____

   _____

2. What kind of behavior would you expect from the **liveliest** puppy in the litter?

   _____

   _____

3. What might you infer about a person who **stammered**?

   _____

   _____

4. What have you been waiting **expectantly** for?

   _____

   _____

5. How have you **demonstrated** your ability to make people laugh?

   _____

   _____

▶ **Write a sentence below using two Critical Vocabulary words.**

   _____

Name _____

Plot

The **plot** of a story is made up of its settings, events, and character development. The plot can be broken into sections called *rising action, climax* or *turning point, falling action,* and *resolution.*

▶ **Reread paragraphs 51–55 in** *Cooper's Lesson.* **Then answer the questions.**

1. What is the setting of the story?

_____

_____

_____

2. How does the setting contribute to the development of the plot?

_____

_____

_____

▶ **Reread pages 348 and 349 to answer the question below.**

3. How does Mr. Lee's character contribute to the plot?

_____

_____

_____

Name _____

Prefixes *in-* and *im-*

The prefixes *in-* and *im-* mean "in" or "into." When a **prefix** is added to the beginning of a base word, it changes the meaning of the word.

> **Complete the chart with words that contain prefixes *in-* and *im-*.**

in-	*im-*

> **Write a sentence for each word in the chart.**

_____

_____

_____

_____

_____

_____

_____

_____

_____

_____

Name _____

Point of View

The **point of view** is who is telling the story. A story can be told by a character in the story. This is **first-person** point of view. If an outside narrator tells the story, it is **third-person** point of view. The point of view an author chooses to tell the story from determines much of what readers learn about the characters and events in the story.

> **▶ Reread paragraphs 1–5 in *Cooper's Lesson* and then answer the questions below.**

1. What point of view does the author use to tell the story?

_____

_____

2. How do you know the story is written from this point of view?

_____

_____

> **▶ After reading *Cooper's Lesson*, answer the questions below about the point of view of the story.**

3. Whose thoughts and feelings do we learn about through the story's narrator?

_____

_____

4. How are readers able to know both Mr. Lee's and Cooper's perspectives in the story?

_____

_____

Unusual Spelling Patterns

▸ **Read each sentence. Write the word from the box that best replaces the underlined word or words in each sentence. Underline the unusual spelling pattern. Circle the sound that the unusual spelling pattern makes.**

research	unbelievable	unguarded	submarine
unpleasant	subtitle	unfortunate	untypical
recycle	disguise	rebuild	refuel

Sentence	Word	Sound
1. Jack's story was so <u>outrageous</u> that we began to laugh.	_____	/ē/ /ō/
2. The city will <u>construct again</u> the monument destroyed by the tornado.	_____	/ĭ/ /ŭ/
3. The diner's food was so <u>yucky</u>, we could not eat it.	_____	/ē/ /ĕ/
4. That behavior is <u>not usual</u> of that kind of animal.	_____	/ĭ/ /ī/
5. Wade was <u>unrecognizable</u> in his costume.	_____	/ĭ/ /ī/
6. The students had to <u>look up</u> information on the topic.	_____	/ər/ /är/
7. The <u>vehicle</u> can travel underwater.	_____	/ă/ /ē/
8. The castle was left <u>without protection</u>.	_____	/ur/ /är/
9. It was <u>unlucky</u> that I missed my plane.	_____	/ĭ/ /ē/
10. Many communities try to <u>reuse</u> certain materials, including paper, glass, plastic, and metal.	_____	/ĭ/ /ī/

Name _____

Author's Craft

Author's craft is the language and techniques authors use to make their stories more interesting. Author's craft techniques also communicate ideas to the reader.

> **Reread paragraphs 20–22 in *Cooper's Lesson* and then answer the questions.**

1. What does "Cooper's heart sank" mean? What does "his tongue lay as heavy and still in his mouth as a dead fish" mean?

_____

_____

2. How do these phrases contribute to the meaning of the text?

_____

_____

> **Reread paragraphs 60–64 in *Cooper's Lesson*. Then answer the questions.**

3. Why does the author use the anecdote?

_____

_____

4. How does the anecdote help readers better understand the characters?

_____

_____

Homophones: Using Context to Determine Meaning

▶ **Choose the correct word to complete each sentence. Write it on the line. Underline the context clue that helped you choose the correct word.**

1. When Grandpa went on a trip, he promised to _____ postcards to us.
   right   write

2. I was so hungry that I _____ four pieces of pizza.
   eight   ate

3. When Katrina was sick, she was _____ from her fever.
   week   weak

4. The _____ wore armor to protect himself and his horse.
   knight   night

5. When we were making the cake, we ran out of _____ .
   flower   flour

6. Juan finished the _____ puzzle by himself.
   hole   whole

7. We had to _____ in line for an hour to buy the tickets.
   wait   weight

8. As Mom was driving, she stepped on the _____ to avoid hitting the squirrel.
   break   brake

9. The weary travelers stayed at a small _____ by the ocean.
   inn   in

10. When we went to camp, we _____ horses.
   road   rode

Name _____

Homophones

> Read each clue. Choose a homophone from the box that matches the context of each clue. Write the word in the puzzle.

chews	toe	rows	peace	hall
waste	piece	jeans	sale	heard
plane	choose	herd	tow	rose
allowed	haul	aloud	plain	sail

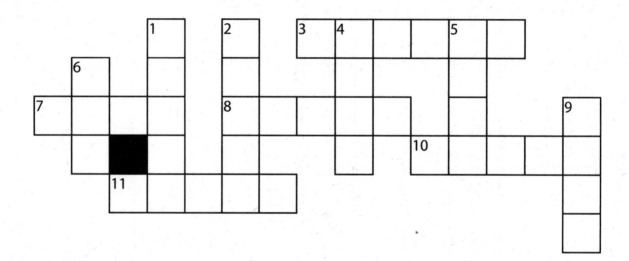

Across	**Down**
3. to pick one thing instead of another	**1.** to throw away things without using them
7. the way crops are planted in fields	**2.** a flat area of level land
8. to say something so others can hear	**4.** to transport goods over distances
10. quiet	**5.** when stores discount their merchandise
11. pants made of heavy cotton	**6.** one of the 10 digits on your feet
	9. a group of cows

Recognize Root Words

▶ **Read each sentence. Underline the word containing a suffix. Write the root word in the first column and the suffix in the second column.**

Sentence	Root Word	Suffix
1. Yesterday was cloudier than today.		
2. That character is the strangest one in the story.		
3. The street was quieter when it became dark.		
4. The youngest person in the family is two years old.		
5. The athlete's breathing was rapid after the race.		
6. The beach is smoother by the ocean.		
7. Mark solved the math problem correctly.		
8. That small knife is the sharpest one.		
9. Are you sure this measurement is accurate?		
10. This puzzle is the easiest one on the shelf.		

Name _____

Recognize Root Words

> **Read each sentence. Circle the word that has a prefix or suffix. Then write the root word on the line.**

1. The storm made swimming dangerous. _____

2. The strongman made weightlifting look effortless. _____

3. We listened closely to the weather report. _____

4. We were able to find a replacement for the part. _____

5. We were uncertain about our science project. _____

6. Liz had many colorful seashells. _____

7. Adam gave the adorable dog a treat. _____

8. She bought the fanciest dress. _____

9. The street crew will remove the snow. _____

10. Uncle Pete was uninjured in the accident. _____

Name _____

Multisyllabic Words with Affixes

▶ Read each sentence. Underline the word that has a prefix or suffix. Then write the word in the correct box, circling the affix.

1. This story is the craziest one I have ever read.

2. Would you untangle this knot for me?

3. The woman gave an incorrect answer on the quiz show.

4. I want to reimagine the event.

5. She accidentally dropped the book.

6. Sean played the piano superbly at the concert.

7. This chair is very uncomfortable.

8. The magician made the rabbit disappear.

Prefix	Suffix

Name _____

Multisyllabic Words with Affixes

> Add one of the following prefixes to each base word to make its opposite.

| in– | dis– | un– | mis– |

easy	
honest	
dependent	
fasten	
identify	

definite	
forgivable	
behave	
represent	
obey	

Choose the word with the correct affixes to fit the meaning.

reheated	rewind	underwater	preheat	misprint	previewed
disable	reviewed	replaying	unable	reprint	unwind

1. to heat before

_____

2. to print wrongly

_____

3. below the water

_____

4. playing again

_____

5. viewed before

_____

6. to wind again

_____

Name _____

Review Syllable Division Patterns

> Read each sentence and look at the clue at the end. Choose the word that makes the most sense in the blank, and write the word on the line. Then divide that word into syllables. You will only use a word one time, and there will be words not used.

V/V	V/CV	VC/V
dial	deny	cabin
fluids	ocean	talent
create	frozen	limit
lion	pilot	novel

1. Many amazing sea creatures live in the _____ . (V/CV)

2. My little brother was scared by the roar of the _____ . (V/V)

3. Last summer, we spent a week in a _____ in the mountains. (VC/V)

4. Could you please turn down the volume by using the _____ ? (V/V)

5. I really enjoyed reading the adventure _____ . (VC/V)

6. She has such musical _____ ! (VC/V)

7. It is important to drink a lot of _____ when you exercise. (V/V)

8. The _____ landed the airplane safely. (V/CV)

9. In art class, we were able to _____ a sculpture with clay. (V/V)

10. The children were ice skating on the _____ pond. (V/CV)

Review Syllable Division Patterns

▷ **Read each sentence. Look at the word choices beneath the sentence, and write the one that would make the most sense on the line. Then draw a line between the syllables in the word you chose.**

1. My favorite food is cheese _____ .
    cherry   pizza   pumpkin

2. I needed to _____ the shirt for a bigger size.
    button   transfer   exchange

3. My dad used the _____ to smooth the surface of the wood.
    sandpaper   slipper   ostrich

4. We could hear the chirp of the _____ in the darkness.
    sandwich   cricket   children

5. Although the sweater was warm, it was very _____ .
    athletic   constant   itchy

6. Our puppy gets into a lot of _____ when left alone.
    mischief   concrete   zipper

7. The smell of baking cookies filled the _____ .
    district   kitchen   neighborhood

8. The _____ jumped high above the waves of the ocean.
    farmer   rabbit   dolphin

Name _____

Compound Words

▶ Read the sentences carefully. Circle the compound word you see in each sentence. After the sentence, write the words that make up the compound word you found.

1. I climbed the staircase to go to my room. _____, _____

2. The toothpaste had a refreshing mint flavor. _____, _____

3. The guard helped the students at the crosswalk. _____, _____

4. The moonlight reflected brightly off the pond. _____, _____

5. When it was time to leave, I waved goodbye. _____, _____

6. Deanna likes to catch fireflies in the summer. _____, _____

7. The teacher wrote the problem on the blackboard. _____, _____

8. My brother's favorite sport is football. _____, _____

9. I felt homesick when I went to camp last summer. _____, _____

10. Could you put this magazine on the bookshelf? _____, _____

Name _____

Multisyllabic Compound Words

> **Read each sentence and the words in the box below. Find a word from the box that makes sense in the sentence, and write it on the line. Write the smaller words that make up the compound word on the lines after the sentence. Then divide these words into syllables.**

underwater	grandmother
fingernails	overdue
sandpaper	fisherman
strawberry	housekeeper
saltwater	screwdriver

1. I spread the gooey _____ jam on my toast. _____, _____

2. Mariah painted her _____ a bright pink color. _____, _____

3. Dad used the _____ to put the new bike together.
_____, _____

4. We went to the library to return the _____ books. _____, _____

5. Many tropical fish live in _____. _____, _____

6. The _____ packed his pole, net, bait, and bucket into the boat.
_____, _____

7. I look forward to visiting my _____ because she is a great cook.
_____, _____

8. Jamal used the _____ to smooth the wood of his bookshelf.
_____, _____

Name _____

Multisyllabic Words

▶ Read each sentence. Circle the multisyllabic word that has a prefix, suffix, or inflectional ending added to a root word. Divide the word into syllables. Then write the root word on the line provided.

1. My dad is fixing the old car. _____

2. Would you like to go bowling? _____

3. The governor rode in the parade. _____

4. We put all of the food in the refrigerator. _____

5. The child said, "Please go away!" _____

6. I quickly ate my lunch. _____

7. The shop had many cute dresses in the window. _____

8. I walk our dog around the block each day. _____

9. My mom used fresh pumpkins to make the pie. _____

10. We had to walk briskly to get to school on time. _____

Multisyllabic Words

▷ Read each sentence and look at the clue at the end. Choose the word that makes the most sense in the blank, and write the word on the line. Then divide that word into syllables. You will only use a word one time, and there will be words not used.

V/CV	VC/V	VC/CV
tiny	never	dinner
crocus	column	index
recite	talent	confess
cement	hazard	sandals

1. The workers poured _____ to make the sidewalk. (V/CV)

2. We ate chicken for _____ yesterday. (VC/CV)

3. What act will you perform for the _____ show? (VC/V)

4. Did you pack a pair of _____ for the beach? (VC/CV)

5. The new mother held her _____ baby. (V/CV)

6. I've _____ seen that TV show. (VC/V)

7. I looked in the _____ of the book. (VC/CV)

8. My mom planted the _____ bulbs in the garden. (V/CV)

9. My dad drove carefully around the _____ in the road. (VC/V)

10. Can you _____ the poem for the class? (V/CV)